Bestselling author of *The Well-Watered Woman*

GRETCHEN SAFFLES

WORD
BEFORE
WORLD

*100 Devotions
to Put Jesus First*

TYNDALE
MOMENTUM®

A Tyndale nonfiction imprint

Visit Tyndale online at tyndale.com.

Visit Tyndale Momentum online at tyndalemomentum.com.

Visit Well-Watered Women at wellwateredwomen.com.

Tyndale, Tyndale's quill logo, *Tyndale Momentum*, and the Tyndale Momentum logo are registered trademarks of Tyndale House Ministries. Tyndale Momentum is a nonfiction imprint of Tyndale House Publishers, Carol Stream, Illinois.

Word before World is a trademark of Life Lived Beautifully LLC.

Word before World: 100 Devotions to Put Jesus First

Designed by Libby Dykstra

Edited by Stephanie Rische

Published in association with William K. Jensen Literary Agency, 119 Bampton Court, Eugene, Oregon 97404.

Unless otherwise indicated, all Scripture quotations are from The ESV® Bible (The Holy Bible, English Standard Version®), copyright © 2001 by Crossway, a publishing ministry of Good News Publishers. Used by permission. All rights reserved.

Scripture quotations marked NLT are taken from the *Holy Bible*, New Living Translation, copyright © 1996, 2004, 2015 by Tyndale House Foundation. Used by permission of Tyndale House Publishers, Carol Stream, Illinois 60188. All rights reserved.

Scripture quotations marked NIV are taken from the Holy Bible, *New International Version,*® *NIV.*® Copyright © 1973, 1978, 1984, 2011 by Biblica, Inc.® Used by permission. All rights reserved worldwide.

Scripture quotations marked BSB are taken from The Holy Bible, Berean Standard Bible, BSB. Copyright © 2016, 2018 by Bible Hub. Used by permission. All rights reserved worldwide.

Scripture quotations marked NASB are taken from the (NASB®) New American Standard Bible,® copyright © 1960, 1971, 1977, 1995, 2020 by The Lockman Foundation. Used by permission. All rights reserved. www.lockman.org.

The URLs in this book were verified prior to publication. The publisher is not responsible for content in the links, links that have expired, or websites that have changed ownership after that time.

For information about special discounts for bulk purchases, please contact Tyndale House Publishers at csresponse@tyndale.com, or call 1-855-277-9400.

Library of Congress Cataloging-in-Publication Data

A catalog record for this book is available from the Library of Congress.

ISBN 978-1-4964-4635-0

Printed in China

30	29	28	27	26	25	24
7	6	5	4	3	2	1

✳

To Carla, for faithfully teaching me to put the Word before the world through Wednesday Bible study, late-night laundry folding, and spur-of-the-moment phone calls

WHEN PUTTING THE WORLD BEFORE THE WORD ISN'T WORKING

The unwelcome chime of my alarm jolts me awake. Still half asleep, I clumsily press the snooze button in the pitch black of our bedroom. In what feels like a matter of seconds, fifteen minutes pass, and the alarm chimes again. This time I grab my phone and tap the internet icon in a stubborn attempt to wake up while remaining in bed—checking email, scrolling social media, perusing news headlines.

By the time I leave the comfort of my covers and place my feet on the carpet, a pit of insecurity has formed in my stomach. The perfectly polished photos I just consumed on social media directly contrast with the unkempt reality before me. On top of that, my mind is racing one hundred miles per hour as I ruminate on a doomsday article I read that has me convinced the world is on the brink of disaster!

Fear strangles my peace, my vision is obstructed by a mountain of worry, and the contentment I could have enjoyed is crushed to smithereens . . . and it's only 6:30 a.m.

This exact scenario has happened more times than I care to admit. When I put the world before the Word of God, the outcome is always the same: I'm left spiritually dry.

One December, on the eve of a new year, I sat down with my journal to get to the bottom of why I was struggling with perpetual discouragement in my faith. As I took inventory of how I spent my time, I discovered a habit of giving Jesus my leftovers. Despite what I said I believed, the ideas, priorities, and pursuits of this world had more authority and influence over the formation of my soul than the Word of God did.

Peace was absent from my mind, anxiety had taken up residence in my soul, and discontentment drove my desires. My spiritual taste buds had become used to the unsatisfying junk food the world offers: surface-level affirmations and quick fixes. I needed to be retrained to crave the satisfying feast of God's Word.

Frustrated by my failure to put Christ first, I confessed my desperate need for the Holy Spirit's help.

I'd tried and failed enough times to recognize that the true pursuit of God is not a self-help journey; it's a Spirit-led surrender as we learn how to savor our Savior above all else. As I realized this, I wrote down a quick phrase to reframe how I wanted to spend my time, start my days, and shape my mindset:

⇢— Word before World —⇠

This three-word statement has become my morning manifesto, my afternoon anthem, and my evening comfort. No matter the season of life I'm in or what circumstances I'm going through, these three words transform my worldview, my schedule, my dreams, and my desires. When my alarm sounds in the morning, I remember: *Word before world*. When I reach for my phone to escape the pressures and stresses of everyday life, the Holy Spirit reminds me: *Word before world*. When my Bible remains unopened for days at a time, I pick it back up and resolve, by God's grace: *Word before world*. Instead of looking at my phone, my lists, and my plans for direction and nourishment, I commit to looking first to Jesus—and this changes everything.

How to Use This Devotional

Anytime is the right time to read the Word of God. This devotional is written and designed with that in mind. You can pick it up at any time of the day, any day of the year for spiritual encouragement, enduring truths to hold on to, and practical ways you can put Jesus first in your everyday life. My aim in writing these words is to point you to *the* Word. Devotionals are not meant to be replacements for Bible study, prayer, or worship; they are tools for spiritual refreshment and reminders of what God's Word says. If you only have time to read one thing, start with Scripture and allow this devotional to be an overflow or extension of your Bible study.

One way to approach this devotional is to think of it as a steroid shot of truth. In moments when your faith wanes and fear rages, open it and read about God's faithfulness. When your desire for God weakens and your craving for the junk food of worldly entertainment increases, pick it up and remind your soul of God's goodness. In the back, you'll find a topical index. Feel free to use it when you are walking through a hard season and need a direct reminder about God's provision for that specific need.

Another way to use this devotional is to read it straight through—for one hundred days or however many days it takes you. Each day begins with a key verse and ends with a statement you can meditate on called "Word before World" and an action step called "Grow in Grace." Within each devotional, I have cited many other Scripture passages. If you desire to go deeper, look up each of these verses in your Bible. You can add extra notes in the margins of your devotional about what they say. You might choose to write the date you are reading the entry, what you are going through, and what God is teaching you so you can reflect on it in the future. Most importantly, bathe your time of study and reading in prayer, talking to God as you put the Word before the world.

Putting Jesus First

The "Word before world" idea originates from John's opening words in his Gospel: "In the beginning was the Word, and the Word was with God, and the Word was God" (John 1:1). Right away, the apostle John shows Jesus' connection with the creation of the world: "In the beginning God created . . ." (Genesis 1:1). Before there was anything—there was God. Jesus, the Son of God, who is the living Word, was also in the beginning, and he created the world through words.

The Word has always come before the world. The apostle Paul elaborates on this same jaw-dropping truth about Jesus: "He is before all things, and in him all things hold together" (Colossians 1:17). Jesus is the Word of God cloaked in human flesh—the one who is, who was, and who is to come (see Revelation 1:8). "Word before world" is how God wired all of creation, and when we treasure his Word above all else and live according to his ways, his Word gives us abundant life in Christ (see Psalm 119:93; John 4:13-14; John 10:10).

My desire in writing this hundred-day devotional is to walk with you as we seek to exalt Jesus above everything, putting him in his rightful place as King of our hearts. God's Word never changes, yet it always changes us. I pray God will use each devotional to help you cultivate a daily rhythm of seeking Jesus, whether you're in a season of joy or a season of sorrow, whether your calendar feels packed or lonely, whether your heart is heavy or light or somewhere in between.

Jesus doesn't change if it's morning, noon, or night, if it's summer, autumn, or winter, if we're old or young, if we're mourning or rejoicing. He is the same yesterday, today, and forever (see Hebrews 13:8), and he is faithful no matter what is happening in your world and in your heart.

When we put God's Word before the world, we will experience fullness of joy, peace that surpasses all understanding, and hope to carry us through any trial (see Psalm 16:10-11; Philippians 4:6-7; and Romans 5:3-5).

When Jesus is first, we will find that everything else falls into its rightful place.

UNCHANGING GOD IN CHANGING SEASONS

The grass withers, the flower fades,
but the word of our God will stand forever.

ISAIAH 40:8

Weather in the South can be frustratingly unpredictable. In the winter, we might enjoy idyllic seventy-degree weather one day, fooling the trees into sprouting early, followed by a day that's overcast, cold, and rainy. Snow is a rare sight, but when we do get a slight dusting, everyone flocks to the store to stock up on bread, milk, and hot chocolate before everything shuts down. In the summer, we might be sweating up a storm in the blistering morning sun, only to huddle indoors in the afternoon watching an ominous thunderstorm blow in.

When my son was in kindergarten, he was delighted when his teacher assigned him the role of class weather watcher. To fulfill his responsibilities, he'd walk over to the window and describe to his classmates what he saw outside. Was the sidewalk wet with rain? Were billowy clouds darkening his view? Was the sun shining brightly? Were small cotton clouds speckling the sky? Ever since his days as weather watcher, he has been fascinated by predictions about what the weather would be like in the days ahead.

I'm just like my son, except I find myself relentlessly watching the weather of my own life, scanning the horizon for what storm might be brewing. I'm eager to know what I should prepare for, what I should bring with me, or whether I should just stay put. Like a traveler packing my bag for a long journey, I want to be prepared for *anything* that could happen.

When it comes to the seasons of nature, my favorite is springtime, hands down. As a gardener, I anxiously await the first post-frost sunny day in April, when I can crack open the dormant soil and plant my prized zinnia seeds. I wish I could live in perpetual springtime, soaking up the days when the sun goes to bed later and we can use nature's air-conditioning, leaving all the windows open. But that is not how life unfolds. We enjoy pleasant seasons and endure harsh ones; we bask in the sunshine and take refuge from the rain; we gaze at clear skies and prepare for cloudy days.

The same is true in my walk with God. I wish I could live in a never-ending season of growth and abundance—enjoying the nearness of God, savoring the sweetness of Scripture, squeezing all the joy out of what comes my way. But just as the seasons of nature change, so do the seasons of life. We can't prepare for every situation we will face or pack for every potential problem. Instead, God calls us to entrust our souls to his tender care (see Proverbs 3:5-6). He sees each crimson leaf that drifts to the ground, each zinnia petal unfolding, each baby bird nestled in a tree. How much more does he see and sustain us?

One thing remains the same in every season—the unchanging character, presence, and provision of God.

In winter seasons, God's Word warms and comforts our souls (see Psalm 119:50). In spring seasons, God's Word awakens and prunes our faith (see John 15:1-2). In summer seasons, God's Word grows and strengthens our endurance (see Psalm 73:26). In autumn seasons, God's Word produces a harvest for his glory (see John 15:8).

Prioritizing the Word before the world cloaks us against the cold of unbelief, shades us from the heat of unexpected trials, nourishes us in droughts of waiting, and satisfies us when answered prayers bloom and abound. The God of every season gives us eternal shelter to enjoy rest through Christ. Instead of being a weather watcher, on the lookout for what we might walk through next, we can dwell in the sanctuary of God's never-changing Word, knowing he will always provide us with the sustaining grace we need to not only survive but to thrive in him.

Word before World

We don't know what tomorrow may hold,
but we know the one who holds tomorrow,
and he is always and forever good.

Grow in Grace

Take a moment to write down what season of life
you're currently in. Does it feel like spring, summer, fall,
or winter in your soul? No matter the season you're
weathering, you can find rest in God's unchanging
promises and the enduring hope in his Word.

FIRST THINGS FIRST

God is able to make all grace abound to you,
so that having all sufficiency in all things at all times,
you may abound in every good work.

2 CORINTHIANS 9:8

Every morning, with heavy eyes and groggy vision, I pour my first cup of coffee. I walk to the couch and sink into the well-worn cushions, sitting in a daze for a few moments, trying to coax my soul out of its slumber. My initial prayer is almost always the same: *God, please wake me up so I can read the Word before I start this day!*

I crave this time—the stillness and quiet, the calm before the storm. I want these first moments to be perfect, peaceful, and perspective-shaping. But instead of being a scene of serenity, these times often look like a string of external interruptions or an internal skirmish.

As my mental distractions grow louder, my phone beckons me from the cabinet where it has been resting all night, silently screaming for me to pick it up and check email or scroll social media for just a minute. But I know that once I open the door, the noise of the world will crank up. I ask the Lord to help me resist the temptation to zone out so I can settle my soul in his unchanging Word.

Miraculously, I open my Bible and journal and soak in God's Word. Sometimes these moments multiply as I feast on Scripture, and other times I am interrupted by early-waking children or a random thought about something important I forgot to do. Sometimes I sense God's presence as tangibly as if he were on the couch with me, and other times I wonder if I am talking to a brick wall. But one thing is certain: I never regret training my soul to put Jesus first.

When you're tempted to choose what's easy instead of what's best for your soul, remember:

* Even when you're tempted to put Jesus behind something else in your life, he will give you more grace to put him first (see 2 Corinthians 12:9).
* Even when it's hard to wake up and get going, he will give you the strength to open your eyes and face each day with confidence in his provision (see Philippians 4:13).
* Even when you choose what's easy instead of opening your Bible, he will give you endurance to keep seeking him (see Hebrews 12:1-2).

When you aim to put Jesus first in your life, expect to face roadblocks that make it hard to press on. The snooze button becomes more enticing, and it is tempting to pick up your phone before picking up your Bible. But take heart, because he who is in you is greater than he who is in the world (see 1 John 4:4)!

The battle in your heart can only be won through Christ's sanctifying work within you as he reframes your desires, rewires your mind, and renews your heart. We do not fight *for* victory but *from* the victory Christ already accomplished on the cross. Christ, who loved you first, will also help you put him first in your day, in your thinking, and in your life.

Show up weak, knowing he is strong. Ask him for strength, knowing he will give you the perseverance to run the race he has set before you. He gives fresh grace from his infinite supply in Christ Jesus, and his mercies are new every morning (see Lamentations 3:22-24)—even on the days when morning comes too soon or you fall asleep in the middle of your Bible reading. Jesus is worthy of your first moments, your last moments, and every moment in between.

When your gaze starts to shift, your mind starts to wander, and your heart starts to lean toward the ways of this world, turn your eyes back to Jesus, who wakes our sleeping souls from their slumber so they awaken to his grace.

Word before World
God's grace helps us put Jesus first,
forgives us when we don't, and keeps us
coming back to him over and over again.

Grow in Grace
What temptation keeps you from opening God's Word?
Confess your need for the Holy Spirit's help to
put the Word before the world today.

PRESSED, BUT NOT CRUSHED

We are pressed on every side by troubles, but we are not crushed.
We are perplexed, but not driven to despair.
We are hunted down, but never abandoned by God.
We get knocked down, but we are not destroyed.

2 CORINTHIANS 4:8-9, NLT

Tucked inside the pages of old books and Bibles on my bookshelf, you'll find the pressings of flowers I've grown or received over the years. When I'm feeling sentimental, I like to peruse the pages and recall memories preserved in time. I've collected small flower pressings from travels, including a tiny white flower from the Garden of Gethsemane and precious wildflowers my boys have plucked from our yard and given to me as gifts. When the petals are pressed between the pages of heavy-duty books, the constant pressure preserves their features and can make them even more beautiful.

After years of collecting flower pressings, I recently arranged some of them between two sheets of glass to hang on the wall of our daughter's room. Each time I pass this piece of art, I'm reminded of God's faithfulness and tender care. He does not crush his loved ones; he presses and preserves us for his glory and our good (see Romans 8:28).

The apostle Paul was well acquainted with affliction. Prior to becoming a Christ-follower, he fiercely persecuted the church. After coming to Christ, Paul found himself on the receiving end of the persecution he'd once carried out.

In his letter to the church at Corinth, Paul reminded believers of the precious, incalculable treasure they held within them: the gospel of Jesus Christ (see 2 Corinthians 4:7-10). He likened their bodies to jars of clay—frail, fragile, temporary, made from dust. At the same time, he reminded them that these jars of clay possess the hope of Jesus, which would preserve them through the sufferings they'd inevitably face as Christians.

Tucked inside this passage, Paul writes these famous words: "We are afflicted in every way, but not crushed; perplexed, but not driven to despair; persecuted, but not forsaken; struck down, but not destroyed" (2 Corinthians 4:8-9). The word *afflicted* more literally means "pressed."[1] Like the flowers I collect and preserve between the pages of my books, we, too, are pressed on all sides yet not crushed. The pressing affliction is for our preservation, our good, and God's glory.

Are you facing a pressing trial right now? Do you feel surrounded by difficulty, assaults from the enemy, and fiery arrows of doubt? Press onward through your Savior, who was pressed on all sides on the cross. Through his death, he destroyed the power of death (see Hebrews 2:14). Through his resurrection, he is now preparing an eternal home for us in heaven (see John 14:23). And one day he will crush Satan once and for all (see Romans 16:20).

When you are pressed on all sides, have courage, because you are being preserved by your Father in heaven. As Paul goes on to say, "We do not lose heart. Though our outer self is wasting away, our inner self is being renewed day by day. For this light momentary affliction is preparing for us an eternal weight of glory beyond all comparison, as we look not to the things that are seen but to the things that are unseen. For the things that are seen are transient, but the things that are unseen are eternal" (2 Corinthians 4:16-18).

We are pressed, but not crushed. Preserved, but not forsaken. Take heart, because God is creating a beautiful work of art out of these trials in your life.

Word before World

Trials will press your faith,
but God will preserve you through it all.

Grow in Grace

When you are pressed on all sides, don't lose heart!
Fix your eyes on the things of heaven, remembering Christ,
who was pressed for you and who gives you victory.

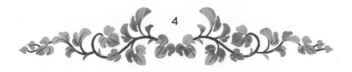

THE RED BIRD'S SERMON

Are not two sparrows sold for a penny? And not one of them will fall to the ground apart from your Father. But even the hairs of your head are all numbered. Fear not, therefore; you are of more value than many sparrows.

MATTHEW 10:29-31

A red bird flits to the barren branch outside the window, cocking its head toward me. For a moment, it looks right at me before promptly flying away. Memories flood my mind: my college dorm room desk, a rickety AC unit outside the fourth-story window, tears streaming down my face, a gnawing ache of hunger in my belly—and a red bird just like this one.

It's not a pretty memory and not one I like to dwell on, but I've grown enough now to hold it without judgment and see it as a redeemed one.

Second semester of my freshman year in college wreaked havoc in my heart. My New Year's resolution was simple: don't gain the dreaded "freshman fifteen." I'm a disciplined person, and with the help of diet books, I succeeded— except not in the way I'd planned. The scale tipped in a downward spiral as I shed pound after pound. By mid-spring, I was a frail version of myself, skin and bones, wondering how I'd dug myself into this pit so quickly. The reflection I saw in the mirror was never good enough. I desperately wanted to believe I was loved and valued, but I was unable to grasp my true identity in Christ.

I remember sitting by my window, alone in my dorm room, with my Bible open and my heart crying out for divine help. I felt so alone, and although I believed in God, I was afraid my brokenness was too deep for him to redeem. But right outside my window, a little red bird perched on the AC unit and looked directly at me.

Tears sprung to my eyes as these words of Jesus came to mind: "Look at the birds of the air: they neither sow nor reap nor gather into barns, and yet your heavenly Father feeds them. Are you not of more value than they? And which of you by being anxious can add a single hour to his span of life?" (Matthew 6:26-27).

As the Word of God ministered to my heart, I began to see that God really did care for me. Over the course of several years, with the help of wise counsel and his healing Word, God redefined my warped perspective on food and body image. Ever since that day, however, the red bird has been a testimony reminding me that God is intimately acquainted with all my ways. He does not leave me starving for grace, wondering if he will provide for my daily needs. He cares about every problem I face. Desperation is not my forever destination; I am satisfied in Christ.

It has been fifteen years since that small red bird preached his sermon to my heart, but that gospel message has never left my soul. God cared then, and he cares now.

He who clothes the flowers of the field also clothes our souls with strength, peace, and purpose. He has done it before, he is doing it now, and he will continue doing so all our days.

When the red bird flits away, the one who created the bird remains.

Word before World

Desperation is not your final destination. God, who cares for the smallest of birds, cares for you and is able to redeem your brokenness.

Grow in Grace

When has God given you a tangible reminder about his provision and care? Look for those reminders as you go about your day, and thank him for noticing all that happens to you—the big things and the small ones.

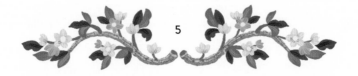

BETTER THAN YOUR BIG DREAMS

I am the true vine, and my Father is the gardener. He cuts off every
branch in me that bears no fruit, while every branch that does
bear fruit he prunes so that it will be even more fruitful.

JOHN 15:1-2, NIV

We purchased our first home in the dead of winter, when the branches were barren and the ground was beige. That spring, I was amazed to see fuchsia petals unfurl on a rosebush in the front garden. The previous owners had planted it there, and now I enjoy the blooms each year, even though I didn't lift a finger to help it grow.

As much as I might wish otherwise, life isn't always filled with blooming flowers. Right next to our flowering rosebush, stubborn weeds grow rampant. Despite our efforts to pull them up, they multiply with fervor, constantly popping up in new places.

Our four-year-old likes to pick the tiny yellow dandelions scattered in the grass and present them to me as a gift. He doesn't know these flowers are actually weeds that choke out the plants we want to thrive. In order for new blooms to flourish, weeds must be uprooted.

When trials pop up in our lives, our faith is tested (see James 1:2-4). Trials come in all shapes and sizes—sometimes packaged as big, life-altering circumstances and other times disguised as daily inconveniences and challenges. In order for blooms of faith to flourish, we need to pluck the weeds of doubt and fear that threaten to crowd out the truth of God's character—that he is with us and for us and will never leave us (see Isaiah 43:1-2).

Just as flowers need sun and water, our budding faith needs to soak in the reality of his presence and his goodness.

When life goes well, Jesus is good.

When your day unravels, Jesus is good.

When your dreams are fulfilled, Jesus is good.

When your hopes are crushed, Jesus is good.

When your fears are overwhelming, Jesus is good.

When blooms flourish, Jesus is good.

When the last leaf drifts to the ground, Jesus is good.

When we plant the truth "Jesus is good" in our hearts, we'll be able to receive the gift of pruning when the master Gardener pulls the weeds from our souls and prunes anything that's holding us back from growth (see John 15:2). And we'll be able to rejoice when we see those tender buds of faith start to sprout.

Jesus is good, and knowing this truth is better than your big dreams.

Word before World

No matter what you face today, remember that
Jesus is forever and always good.

Grow in Grace

Take an honest look at the garden of your soul.
What weeds do you see there? What would it
take to pull them out, by God's grace?

EVERY THOUGHT IS AN ARROW

*Humble yourselves, therefore, under the mighty hand of God
so that at the proper time he may exalt you, casting all
your anxieties on him, because he cares for you.*

1 PETER 5:6-7

It was an all-out, knockdown fight to focus my mind during my Bible study this morning. Worries, fears, unresolved questions, and pressing to-dos inundated my mind like water rushing past a broken dam. Every verse I read seemed to stream through one ear and out the other. I huffed a sigh of defeat as the clock relentlessly ticked down the minutes. I knew it wouldn't be long until I was interrupted by a family member and my time studying the Word would end.

In an act of desperation, I scribbled in my journal every thought engulfing my mind in an attempt to wrangle each one into submission. As I put pen to paper and recorded the worries swirling in my head, something unexpected happened.

By the time I set down my pen and read through what I'd written, I realized that every thought pointed like a blinking arrow right back to my need for Jesus. Though my wrestling match felt like a dead end, it actually led to my desired destination: a heart and mind surrendered to Jesus and settled in his Word (see Psalm 119:105).

God is able to turn our distractions into detours directing us to our Savior. Time spent wrestling before, during, and after you read your Bible isn't a waste; it's a way back to him.

When the disappointments of yesterday overshadow your soul, let them remind you to let go of the past and hold fast to the Lord, who makes a way in the wilderness and streams in the desert (see Isaiah 43:19).

When grief over a loss overwhelms you, let your tears allow you to experience the comfort of God as you share in Christ's sufferings (see Psalm 34:18; 2 Corinthians 1:4; Philippians 3:10).

When a struggle with sin rages inside you, allow the Holy Spirit to urge you toward confession, repentance, and restoration (see Romans 2:4; John 16:8).

When unfulfilled longings unsettle you, surrender them to Jesus, who fills every hungry soul with good things (see Psalm 107:9; John 6:35).

There is no wasted time when we wrestle our thoughts into submission to Christ and seek to fill our minds with God's inexhaustible Word. Wrestling is where the sanctification of our souls takes place.

Don't allow the enemy a foothold in your mind, sister. Wrestle with your wayward thoughts and cast all your anxieties on the Lord. Turn your attention to him, and allow every thought to redirect your mind and remind you to trust his Word more deeply.

Word before World

Every distracting thought is an arrow pointing you
back to Christ and your need for him.

Grow in Grace

Set a timer for five minutes and write down every
worry and distracting thought. When the time
is up, review each thought and worry, and identify
how each one points you to your need for Christ.

READ, WORSHIP, REPEAT

I will meditate on your precepts and fix my eyes on your ways.
I will delight in your statutes; I will not forget your word.

PSALM 119:15-16

It's a daily struggle to love God in the midst of mundane, repetitive tasks. The dishes need washing, the laundry needs folding, the trash cans need emptying, hungry bellies need filling—and I find myself inserting the discipline of studying my Bible into this list. At times, meeting with God becomes a "have to" instead of a "get to," a task to check off instead of a delight to partake in.

Our souls need to be reminded of the same promises of God, day after day. We forget what we read, sometimes within seconds of closing our Bibles. Our minds need the kind of renewal that can come only through drinking the refreshing water of the Word (see John 4:14). We need the light of Christ to shine in the darkness of our circumstances (see 2 Corinthians 4:6). We need the reminder that the God who spoke billions of stars into existence is the same God who speaks to us in Scripture (see Psalm 147:4; Isaiah 40:26). The consistent act of reading the Bible engraves truth into the fibers of our being, verse by verse.

True to his Word, the Son of God does not fail us or forsake us (see Deuteronomy 31:6; Psalm 9:10). God has caused his Son, Jesus, to shine on our darkened hearts with the light of the gospel, just as the sun illuminates the darkness of this world each morning.

Think about this stunning reality: you and I did absolutely nothing to cause the sun to rise today, and yet we can fellowship with the one who did. G. K. Chesterton pondered God's faithfulness in the mundane: "For grown-up people are not strong enough to exult in monotony. But perhaps God is strong enough to exult in monotony. It is possible that God says every morning, 'Do it again' to the sun; and every evening, 'Do it again' to the moon. It may not be automatic necessity that makes all daisies alike; it may be that God makes every daisy separately, but has never got tired of making them. It may be that He has the eternal appetite of infancy; for we have sinned and grown old, and our Father is younger than we."[1]

God knows our lives are filled with repetitive tasks. He does not despise the mundane, and neither should we. In fact, God knows that our ordinary tasks are often the very means he uses to refine us and shape us to be more like him.

A deep love for God comes not through reading Scripture one time but through a lifetime of consistently drinking in his Word. The sun and the moon remind us of God's faithfulness to "do it again," every single day.

As you wake up each morning and remember that you did absolutely nothing to cause the sun to rise, God grants you the endurance to open your Bible and read the Word once more. And he often surprises us with delight as we meet him on those pages.

Word before World
Endless delight awaits us as we read God's Word again and again.

Grow in Grace
Do it again today. Open the Word and soak in
the Son's promises as he transforms what might
otherwise seem mundane into worship.

THE BEST PART

From the rising of the sun to its setting,
the name of the LORD is to be praised!
PSALM 113:3

ave you ever taken a picture of a sunrise or sunset only to be left
frustrated by the quality of the image? A photo can never fully do
justice to the beauty we behold with our eyes.

On a trip to Big Sur, California, my husband, Greg, and I witnessed one
of the most breathtaking sunsets I've ever seen. We were driving down
the Pacific Coast Highway when the bright blue sky changed to magnifi-
cent shades of Creamsicle and coral. When I couldn't capture a non-blurry
image of the sky from our moving car, I started to feel panicky. I urged Greg
to pull off the road so I could get a photo before the colors vanished. He
swerved off at the next exit and pulled into a sandy parking lot. I jumped
out of the car with our camera in hand, sprinting to the beach.

Every few steps, I'd stop and snap a few shots, afraid I would miss the
best part. None of the pictures I took compared to the wispy watercolor
clouds reflecting on the ocean waves. *Click, click, click*—I couldn't stop taking pictures and recording videos as I tried in vain to catch the seagulls
swooping in the sky, the fishing boats bobbing in the sea, and the rays of
light streaming from the setting sun.

But I kept coming up short. After a few minutes, the sky darkened and its brilliant colors faded to deep indigo. We walked back to the car, emptied our shoes of sand, and continued the drive to our hotel.

As I flipped through the photos I'd taken, my heart sank. Instead of enjoying God's masterpiece—the waves crashing before me, the infinite golden sand beneath my feet, and the colors of the sky—I had been consumed with trying to take the best picture. I had missed the best part.

In Psalm 113, a psalm of praise, the psalmist declares there is not a single moment in the day when God is not worthy of praise. Rather than attempt to capture or contain God's greatness, the writer overflows with adoration. He begins his psalm with a declaration to praise the Lord and ends in the same posture of adoration. The sun follows the same pattern as it rises and sets each day, reminding us to begin and end our days with praise.

As we behold the beauty of God in Scripture and in creation, our hearts are sparked to praise his name, both now and forever. Every sunrise, every sunset beckons us to set aside distractions to enjoy the best part—praising our faithful, righteous, steadfast, glorious God.

When we root our lives in praise and fix our eyes on him, we won't miss the best part, because the best part is knowing and praising him—no camera required.

Word before World

We won't miss the best parts in life when our eyes are set on beholding Jesus in the Word and glimpsing his grace in the world.

Grow in Grace

Next time you see a sunrise, instead of grabbing your phone or camera to capture the moment, simply watch and praise God, who is faithful from the rising to the setting sun—and every moment in between.

9

GUIDED BY YOUR GOOD SHEPHERD

I am the good shepherd. I know my own and my own know me,
just as the Father knows me and I know the Father;
and I lay down my life for the sheep.

JOHN 10:14-15

Four weeks after having my third baby, I was admitted to the hospital for mysterious stomach pain. For five long days, my body was poked, prodded, and tested as doctors searched for the root cause of my illness. After I was finally discharged, the dark clouds of depression overshadowed my soul. During this season, I clung to every word in Psalm 23 like a lifeboat. For months I rehearsed each verse of this psalm, etching it deeper into the grooves of my mind.

Psalm 23 was more than a comforting blanket to wrap my shivering soul in; it was oxygen to my spiritual lungs that were struggling to breathe. One day I wrote this psalm in my own words as a raw declaration to my heart that my Shepherd will never leave my side.

At some point, shadows will inevitably darken the path we take. But the Good Shepherd never leaves his sheep to fend for themselves (see John 10:14-15).

Read the words of my paraphrase slowly. Allow God's Word to soothe your soul with the gospel promise that Jesus, the Good Shepherd, protects you, defends you, cares for you, and invites you to find rest in him.

* * *

The Lord is my Shepherd; I lack no good thing. In the morning, in the evening, in the darkness of the night, and in the middle of the day, he is with me—even when I don't feel his presence.

He makes me lie down in green pastures, even when I don't want to stop and rest. He knows what's best, even when I think I know better. He invites me to embrace my limits and enjoy shelter in his tender care. He leads me beside still waters; he refreshes my worn-out soul.

He leads me on the roadway of righteousness toward his eternal Kingdom—all for his name's sake. Everything my Shepherd does is according to his character. He never contradicts himself, and he is always good. As I walk these winding, lonely paths, I encounter shadows that threaten my peace and joy. They are terrifying in the moment, but they are just shadows. A shadow can't hurt me when I'm covered by God's grace.

So I won't fear evil, because my Good Shepherd is with me. He comforts me, corrects me, and restores me with his rod and his staff. He even prepares a feast for me at his table in the presence of my enemies! The truest feast is found in his presence. His Word nourishes my soul.

Surely his goodness and his mercy will chase after me and accompany me on this journey—every day, every moment, every second of my life. One day I will dwell with him forever in the new heaven and new earth, where there are no more dark shadows, where there is no more fear or pain (see Revelation 21:1-4).

Until then, I'll walk with my Shepherd, follow my Shepherd, and trust my Shepherd, who became like me, a sheep—the Lamb who was slain for my redemption (see John 1:29; Revelation 13:8).

There's no greater love than my Shepherd's love and no greater sacrifice than his (see John 15:13).

Yes, the Lord is my Shepherd. I lack no good thing, because I have everything I need in him.

Word before World
Jesus is our Good Shepherd, who provides
for and cares for his beloved sheep.

Grow in Grace
Set aside five to ten minutes to feast your mind on
Psalm 23 and find rest for your soul. You might even
paraphrase the psalm in your own words, like I did.

GOD

IS NOT AFRAID

OF YOUR DOUBTS

THE WAITING PLACE

For God alone my soul waits in silence;
from him comes my salvation.

PSALM 62:1

When I was a girl, starting around April, I would wish away the days leading up to summer. I couldn't *wait* until school let out so I could begin my two months of long bike rides, frequent pool visits, and late nights spent catching fireflies.

Now that I'm an adult, the hot summer months aren't as appealing. I find that I'm just as antsy for the next season when the summer heat lingers too long. By the time September rolls around, I'm itching for chilly mornings and comforting soups for dinner, even though where I live we will likely be sporting shorts and sandals until mid-November. When the heat is reluctant to leave, my desire for cooler temperatures overtakes the joy of the season I'm in. But once the long-awaited cold months arrive, I find myself pining for spring.

The changing of the seasons always affects my outlook. Even though I should know by now that the shift is gradual, there's still a persistent longing in my soul to officially be fully immersed in a new season, to pack up my shorts and pull out my sweaters or to toss aside my sandals and exchange them for boots.

Just as I grumble impatiently under my breath when a meteorological season lingers longer than I'd like, I do the same with seasons of life I wish would pass. The in-between—the waiting place—is often the hardest place to be. I struggle to make peace with circumstances that change slowly while the present discomfort holds on tight.

Seasons come and go—some fast and some slow—because life is constantly shifting and causing shifts in us. In the midst of our waiting places, God is teaching us to see him at work, savor his presence, sit still, and trust his provision (see Psalm 27:14). Tomorrow isn't ours, and neither is the next season; we only have today (see Matthew 6:34). And in the midst of this day, in this season, God is just as faithful as he has ever been.

God is faithful today, just as he was when Abraham and Sarah waited twenty-five long years for the impossible pregnancy God promised (see Genesis 12:1-7; 21:5).

He is faithful in our waiting place, just as he was when the Israelites trekked in the wilderness for forty years on their way to the Promised Land (see Deuteronomy 8:2).

He is faithful in seasons of slow change, just as he was when Paul desired to reach Rome during his missionary journeys but was stopped multiple times (see Romans 1:13).

No matter the season you are in, God is just as faithful today as he was yesterday and as he will be tomorrow (see Hebrews 13:8).

When you find yourself in a waiting place, remind your soul to slow down, settle in, and believe that he is God and he is good—in every slow-changing season.

Word before World

Even when you remain in a waiting place for longer than
you'd prefer, you can trust that God is at work and will
give you the endurance you need to persevere.

Grow in Grace

Make a list of ways God has been faithful in the past, both to you
personally and in Scripture. Tape this list to the front of your Bible
(or in a place you will regularly see it) as a reminder that even
when the changing of seasons is slow, God never changes.

LET THERE BE . . .

In the beginning,
God created the heavens and the earth.
GENESIS 1:1

In the beginning, God created the world with words. "Let there be . . ." unleashed unbounded potential as God painted the canvas of creation. Everything around us is a result of God's creativity—worms burrowing in the soil, lavender skies blanketing a sunrise, kaleidoscope colors tinting leaves. Genesis 1 tells us that God said, God saw, God called, God made, and God blessed—all with his life-giving words.

But God didn't end his masterpiece with the massive elephant weighing up to 15,000 pounds. He didn't stop after designing the ladybug, whose spots protect it from predators. He didn't finish after forming the garden snail, whose mouth contains more than 10,000 microscopic teeth.

The crowning glory of creation was the formation of man and woman in his own image (see Genesis 1:26). Taking dust from the ground, God formed the first man, Adam. He breathed the breath of life into his nostrils, filling Adam's lungs with oxygen. Later, he took a rib from Adam's side and fashioned a wife for him. The pair delighted in each other, enjoying perfect unity with God in the Garden: "God saw everything that he had made, and behold, it was very good" (Genesis 1:31).

I often find myself wishing the story stopped there, with Adam and Eve enjoying a life free from entanglement to shame, walking with their Maker in the cool of the day in an untarnished home. But the serpent showed up like a thief, with cunning words of deception. Adam and Eve believed the serpent and ate the forbidden fruit from the tree of the knowledge of good and evil. Their disobedience robbed God's first Garden of innocence. Where God declared, "Let there be" light and life, Satan brought death with his question "Did God really say?" (Genesis 3:1, NIV).

Did God's Word lose its power when Satan sowed seeds of doubt in the hearts of Adam and Eve? Did God's Word change after their eyes were opened to their nakedness and they wrapped themselves in fig leaves? No. The same God who created with words is the same God who called Adam and Eve out of hiding and then spoke the first gospel promise: a Savior would come through the offspring of a woman, and he would crush the serpent, Satan, finally and forever (see Genesis 3:15).

The Word of God did not lose its power when sin darkened the hearts of Adam and Eve. Hebrews 4:12 describes the Word of God as living and active—pulsing with abundant life, breathing eternal hope into our souls, cutting to the core of our inmost being. The words of Satan seek to destroy; the Words of God always bring life (see John 10:10).

Every verse of Scripture still speaks "let there be" through Christ, the Word (see John 1:1) who made everything.

Word before World

God's Word cuts to the core of our souls, creates life
within us, and crushes the schemes of Satan.

Grow in Grace

How has Satan tempted you to believe God's Word has
lost its power? Preach this truth to your heart: the Savior
has come, proving that God's Word is fully true.

12

TREASURES

Where your treasure is,
there your heart will be also.

MATTHEW 6:21

The air is heavy with dust and memories trapped in time. My eyes scan the messy piles of antiques at the flea market, and all I see are treasures waiting to be mined—heaps of old plates and boxes with trinkets and throwaways. The single competitive bone in my body wakes up, fearing someone might make their discovery before I do.

The owner of the booth, a kind and generous elderly man, loves to tell stories. I listen as I keep searching and eventually dig up some vintage plates from a pile. "How much?" I ask.

"Fifteen dollars for all three," he says.

"You've got a deal," I say, handing him three five-dollar bills and planning how I'll hang these treasures in our home.

* * *

When I was a little girl, I had a ritual every time we visited my grandparents in Arkansas. I'd steal away from the rest of the family and search through all the drawers that weren't off-limits. I vividly remember opening the drawers, one by one, in search of priceless treasures.

The last time I stepped foot in that house was more than a decade ago, but I regularly dream I'm back there, searching the drawers and closets for the shimmer of treasured memories, the comfort of belonging, the riches of family heritage. These heirlooms are reminders to me that life is fleeting but God is forever faithful.

* * *

Seated on a hillside, Jesus gave a message we refer to as the Sermon on the Mount. In these words, he warned his followers not to lay up treasures on earth that can be destroyed in the blink of an eye. Instead, Jesus instructed his followers to store up treasures in heaven, where rust cannot tarnish them, fire cannot consume them, and disaster cannot destroy them (see Matthew 6:19-24).

With this in mind, what should we do with these earthly finds? We hold them loosely while holding tightly to the eternal treasures in the Kingdom to come. The things of earth point us to the real treasure we hunger for—the shimmering gospel truth that God sees redemption where we see rubbish.

* * *

The thrill of a flea market find fades, but the thrill of finding Christ is forever. After all, it's not earthly treasures we're really after; it is what they mean, what they point to—the ultimate treasure of knowing Christ.

Word before World
The things of earth will pass away,
but treasures in heaven last for all eternity.

Grow in Grace
What earthly treasures are you most likely to store up?
What do these treasures reveal about your heart?
What would it look like to treasure Christ
while holding your belongings loosely?

ADD AND SUBTRACT LIKE JESUS

He must become greater and greater,
and I must become less and less.

JOHN 3:30, NLT

Ever have one of those days where you feel like a total failure? Maybe you always seem to be a step or two behind, desperately trying to get your footing, only to stumble again and again? When I have days like these, tears build up inside me and no amount of effort can keep them from overflowing. Like a bathtub filled to the brim, they eventually splash to the floor, and I'm left cleaning up a slippery mess.

Sometimes our most dangerous stumbling blocks are our own expectations. When seasons of life change, bringing new responsibilities and roles, we are often unwilling to let go of what was important in the past to make room for what we're called to today.

For most of my life, I've had the bad habit of adding to my schedule without being willing to subtract something to make room for the new responsibility. Eventually, the math doesn't add up and I am overcommitted and overtired. I've overlooked what Jesus has called me to do in my current season.

Maybe you've been there too—or maybe you're there right now. Your schedule is overflowing, and every minute there's something that needs to be tended to, someone who needs you, somewhere you need to be. You know this pace is unsustainable, but you don't know how to press pause, hit the reset button, and receive the rest Jesus offers.

A life of abundance is not achieved by doing more, accomplishing more, or getting more done. A life of abundance is found when we abide in Christ, receiving all we need for life and godliness in him (see John 15:5).

Flourishing happens when Christ increases in us while our sinful desires decrease. Does this mean we cease to be? In a sense, yes. And in another sense, no. As the love and hope of Christ increase in us, our self-centeredness and pride decrease. At the same time, his character shapes and sharpens ours, so our lives produce gospel fruit (see Galatians 5:22-23).

When you reach the end of your rope, consider that feeling of desperation a gift of grace from God. He sees and collects the tears that spill from our weary eyes (see Psalm 56:8). He does not call us to strive to achieve more through our own efforts, to keep up with those around us, or to get ahead. He calls us to sit at his feet, soak in his Word, release our unrealistic expectations, and find in Jesus the grace and guidance we desperately need (see Luke 10:38-42).

The Christian life is a paradox. In him, we are broken yet healed, empty yet filled.

If the path to dying to self and living for Christ requires that we fail and feel the repercussions of unrealistic expectations, let it be. If it requires us to surpass our limits so we can return to a place of total surrender to Jesus, let it be.

It is worth it to fail in the world's eyes so we can live fully and freely in Jesus.

This is the kind of gospel math we read about in John 3:30: he must increase, we must decrease.

Word before World
More Jesus + less me = life abundantly

Grow in Grace
Write down one thing that needs to be subtracted from your life right now. Now write down one thing that needs to be added in order to seek Jesus and live like him. Ask God to help you discern what commitments are part of the work he has called you to in your current season of life.

14

HOW LONG, O LORD?

How long, O LORD? Will you forget me forever?
How long will you hide your face from me?

PSALM 13:1-2

How long, O Lord?

It's an honest question we've all asked at one point or another. *How long* will I be single? *How long* will I be without a child in my womb? *How long* will I battle depression? *How long* will I be trapped in a prison of anxiety? *How long* will I face these crushing debts? *How long* will I endure this unrelenting physical pain?

When my first son was one year old, I had my first major panic attack—on a plane. At the time, I had no idea the bodily sensations I was feeling were anxiety-related. In the ensuing weeks and months, my body and brain remained in a hypervigilant state, paralyzed by fear. When depression set in and started strangling my joy, I joined King David, the author of Psalm 13, in asking this question. On one particularly crushing day, I curled up in the fetal position in our hand-me-down armchair. The house was empty, and so was my soul. I wept as I read this psalm aloud. These words didn't make my depression go away, but they became a safe haven and source of steadfast hope when darkness descended on my life.

In Psalm 13, King David asks the Lord, "How long?" four different times, exposing his inner wrestling and questioning. David felt forgotten, forsaken, alone, overcome with sorrow, defeated by his enemy, and shaken to the core. Rather than hiding his hurt from the Lord or trying to soften his questions and make them more "appropriate," he came before God just as he was—shattered and baring his wounded soul with raw honesty.

In these six short but theologically jam-packed verses, David transitions from despair to praise. After presenting his laments to God, he says, "But I have trusted in your steadfast love; my heart shall rejoice in your salvation" (verse 5). David moves past "How long?" by focusing on who God is and rejoicing in the ever-present hope of his salvation. He can sing in the midst of his suffering because he knows God has been good to him and will not forsake him.

When "How long?" is all you can mutter, God listens (see Psalm 40:1). Christ endured the pain piercing our hearts. He carried the burdens breaking our souls. He faced the darkness clouding our vision, and he received the punishment for our rebellion (see Isaiah 53). Because of Jesus, we can ask "How long?" and say with confidence, "But I have trusted in your steadfast love; my heart shall rejoice in your salvation" (Psalm 13:5).

Your circumstances may not change, and you may still wonder how much longer you'll bear the burden you carry, but God has the power to change your heart and lift the load. When you are at your lowest, God is still on his throne (see Psalm 47:8). He comes near to mend your broken heart (see Psalm 34:18). You can sing a song of praise, even when the question "How long?" lingers in the back of your mind.

Romans 8:32 says, "He who did not spare his own Son but gave him up for us all, how will he not also with him graciously give us all things?" Just as God didn't forsake his Son when he was hanging on the cross, he will never forsake you.

Word before World
The suffering we face will not last forever;
the steadfast love of the Lord lasts forever.

Grow in Grace
What are you asking "How long?" about right now?
Read Psalm 13. Ask "How long?" with King David, and
remind your soul of the Lord's ultimate salvation.

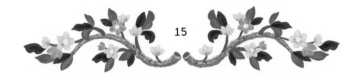

15

WHEN MOUNTAINS DON'T MOVE

*Every valley shall be lifted up, and every mountain
and hill be made low; the uneven ground shall
become level, and the rough places a plain.*

ISAIAH 40:4

What do you do when the mountain your soul longs to see moved . . . doesn't move?

How do you respond when you pray long and hard, staring at the mountain you want to come down, but it stays in its place? What do you do when this mountain blocks your view and you're afraid to move forward or backwards? What do you believe about God when that mountain obstinately refuses to budge?

We pray and sing for the mountains to be moved, but let's be honest: Have you ever seen an actual mountain crumble or step aside? Not a literal one, perhaps, but a metaphorical one? The mountains of our struggles aren't always removed the way we desire, so we give up and become rooted in our fear, doubt, worry, and discouragement. But what if God is actually moving mountains much bigger than the ones we can see—the mountains of our hearts?

After a traumatic experience involving my health a few years ago, I was faced with a terrifying mountain. No matter what I did, this mountain of anxiety refused to budge from in front of me. It prompted me to pull back from community and made me afraid to place my trust in God. I prayed for this mountain to collapse. I begged God to remove it. But he showed me another way to move past this mountain in my heart: to walk over it. To face it for what it was, with him before me, beside me, behind me, and all around me (see Isaiah 43:2). He showed me it was possible to walk over the mountain, step by step, as the fear in my soul bowed down to the maker of the mountains.

Fear cannot be avoided or escaped; it must be faced head on with the hope of the gospel. Even if the mountains don't move, we can walk over them with the fear of God strengthening our hearts. We may do so with trembling hearts, but we walk forward in hope (see Hebrews 11:1).

Some mountains were never meant to be removed; they were meant to be hiked and conquered with God's strength as we learn to trust the one whose love never fails (see Romans 8:37-39).

So let's hike, friends. When the mountains don't move, put on your climbing gear and move forward in faith, freedom, and the victory Jesus died to make ours.

Word before World

Even when the mountain you're facing won't move,
God will give you the strength to move forward
and trek over it by faith.

Grow in Grace

What mountain are you facing today?
Pray the words of Isaiah 40:4, and believe that God,
who made the mountains, can move the mountains.
And he is with you as you hike over the
mountains that don't move.

16

WHAT IS YOUR SCHEDULE TELLING YOU?

Teach us to number our days
that we may gain a heart of wisdom.

PSALM 90:12

Most days, my to-do list doesn't match the amount of time I've allotted to complete it. If you were to peek into my planner, it would quickly become apparent that I believe I'm an exception to the "everyone has only twenty-four hours in a day" rule.

Take yesterday, for example. I was like a ping-pong ball, bouncing from one activity to the next. After scrambling to get my kids ready for school and then dropping them off, I rushed home to attend a meeting for work. After the meeting, I grabbed a snack and joined another meeting, hurrying to get my work done, run errands, and prep dinner—all before school pickup. Just when I thought I had a moment to catch my breath, I'd glance at my schedule and be propelled into the air again, hoping I would land at each intended destination. By nighttime, I was exhausted, beat, kaput. And still, after all the striving, all the coffee consumed, all the pep talks I'd given myself to just keep going, I ended the day with unfinished items on my to-do list. The humbling reality is that like everyone else, I only have twenty-four hours in a day.

But these impossible standards are not put there by God, as if he were tapping his foot, waiting on us to complete our impossible agenda. He knows our limitations. He knows we are human. And when we surrender our schedules to him and commit to doing all that is before us for his glory, he shows us his priorities so we can order our day in a way that leaves us fulfilled rather than exhausted.

No matter your background, location, ambitions, or vocation, every human experiences the same limitation each day: *time*—twenty-four hours, 1,440 minutes, 86,400 seconds, to be exact. Even Jesus, the Son of God, experienced the constraints of time while on earth.

The Gospel writers—Matthew, Mark, Luke, and John—describe how Jesus spent his time through firsthand accounts of his ministry. He proclaimed the gospel of the Kingdom of God, healed those with physical limitations, stopped midjourney to talk to outcasts, ate supper with sinners, made breakfast with his disciples, and even took naps. On a trek through Samaria, Jesus explained to his disciples the mission that shaped his time on earth: "My food is to do the will of him who sent me and to accomplish his work" (John 4:34).

Jesus is our best role model when it comes to time management. His life sheds light on how we can live with eternal vision and a gospel-centered mission.

If you were to dissect the way you spend your time, would it line up with the example set by Jesus?

We might say we don't have time to read the Bible, but our phone's screen time tracker tells us otherwise.

We might say we don't have the capacity to memorize Scripture, but the number of songs and quotes we can retrieve from the recesses of our brain disproves this.

We might say we can't focus during prayer, but our tendency to worry and ruminate reveals our ability to think about one thing, even while doing another task.

The truth is, the way we spend our time reveals what we treasure most (see Matthew 6:21). Jesus' number-one priority was to accomplish the work his Father sent him to do, and this informed the way he spent his time. God created us to live within the boundaries of time, and he gives us the exact amount of time we need to accomplish what he has called us to do.

The same God who took on flesh not only understands the constraints of time but also grants us the wisdom, through his Word, to guide us as we make decisions about how we use the minutes we've been given (see James 1:5).

Your life is always preaching a sermon about what your heart treasures most. What sermon will your schedule preach today?

Word before World
God made us to live within the boundaries of time,
and we can learn from Jesus' example to use the hours
and minutes we've been given to his glory.

Grow in Grace
Review your daily and weekly routines.
What does your schedule reveal about
what your heart treasures? How can you
order your schedule to revolve around Jesus?

17

RUN TO JESUS

It is you who light my lamp; the LORD my God lightens my darkness.
For by you I can run against a troop, and by my God I can leap over
a wall. This God—his way is perfect; the word of the LORD
proves true; he is a shield for all those who take refuge in him.

PSALM 18:28-30

I'm a runner. Not in the physical sense, although I do occasionally lace up my tennis shoes and go for a slow jog. No, I'm a runner in the spiritual sense. For most of my life, I've had the habit of running as far away from my problems, fears, and worries as I possibly can.

Are you a runner too?

When your heart is overwhelmed, do you run to your phone or to food in search of a mental escape?

When insecurity squashes your confidence, do you run to a family member or a friend for encouragement and affirmation?

When discouragement disrupts your peace, do you run to your achievements to validate your worth?

When you are left out of a friend's plans, do you run to a store to shop for something new to numb feelings of loneliness?

King David was a runner. In Psalm 18, he shows us a better place to run to in our time of need. In this psalm, David describes how God delivered him from his enemies. This song mirrors the one he sings later in life, right before his death (see 2 Samuel 22). The myriad trials David faced taught him that nothing this world has to offer would satisfy the longings of his soul.

In Psalm 18:2, King David describes the Lord as "my rock and my fortress and my deliverer, my God, my rock, in whom I take refuge, my shield, and the horn of my salvation, my stronghold." As he proclaims to his soul the character of God, David shows us a better place to run in our distress: the Lord.

David's son Solomon writes a similar truth in Proverbs 18:10: "The name of the LORD is a strong tower, the righteous man runs into it and is safe." There is power in the name of the Lord—power to save, power to shield us from the enemy's attacks, and power to provide a safe haven when storms loom (see Romans 10:13).

We don't need to run away from our problems, because God has given us a better place to run *to*: himself. In his name, we find safety and strength.

Because of Jesus, we don't have to run away from our fears or nagging insecurities. We don't have to flee our problems or avoid our shortcomings. Rather, we can face them with confidence, knowing the Lord will provide endurance, perseverance, and deliverance (see James 1:2-4). Taking refuge in God is better than relying on any false shelter the world has to offer (see Psalm 20:7).

If this is where you find yourself today—if you've laced up your spiritual running shoes and you're furiously fleeing your problems—Christ offers you a better invitation. Your problems are not bigger than God. So unlace your running shoes and find rest in him (see Psalm 46:10).

Run to Jesus today—for help, peace, security, and belonging. As you run toward him, take comfort in knowing that he's running after you too (see Psalm 23:6).

Word before World
God has given us a better place to run to in our time of need—himself.

Grow in Grace
Who or what do you run to when your soul feels burdened?
The next time you're tempted to run away from your
problems, fears, or worries, run *to* your Savior.

18

PRAY RIGHT AWAY

Pray in the Spirit at all times, with every kind of prayer and petition.
To this end, stay alert with all perseverance in your prayers for all the saints.

EPHESIANS 6:18, BSB

"I'm praying for you."

This simple statement goes a long way ... when we follow through. But sometimes I'll say this to a friend as a mere sentiment, convincing myself, *It's the thought that counts*, when in reality, it's the prayer that makes a difference.

In an effort to make sure I actually pray for someone when I say I will, I've made it a practice to pray right away when someone entrusts me with the cares of her heart. Rather than listening and offering my own advice or merely saying, "I'll pray for you," I offer to join my friend in petitioning God right then. When we really believe he is with us, he hears us, and he answers prayer (see 1 John 5:14-15), we are motivated to embrace the gift of coming directly into his presence with our requests.

This might look like praying in a public setting or sending a prayer through a text message or putting a handwritten letter in the mail. Other times it might involve sending a voice memo, making a phone call, or pausing to pray in my living room for my friend as the Holy Spirit brings her to mind.

When I began this practice of praying right away, I didn't realize how the blessing would boomerang back and change me. The more I've made it a habit to intercede and pray for others, the less I worry about myself (see Philippians 4:6-7).

Committing to praying for others is like holding a megaphone to our ears

42

and hearing the gospel message preached to our own weary hearts. Prayer changes us—the way we see, the way we work, what we love, and where we place our hope. Prayer isn't about getting things from God; it's about being conformed to his will (see Psalm 37:4). When we praise God for his faithfulness, petition him for his help, and press into his promises, our confidence grows and our peace multiplies (see Psalm 9:1-2; Hebrews 4:16).

Becoming a faithful prayer warrior doesn't happen overnight; it happens one prayer at a time. You don't need eloquent, repetitive words in order to come to God in prayer (see Matthew 6:5-8). You already have the Word of God, and Scripture holds the most powerful words we can pray. As a Christ-follower, you've been gifted with the Holy Spirit to help you, guide you, protect you, and pray on your behalf (see Romans 8:26-27). Because of Christ's work on the cross, you can come before God anytime, anywhere in prayer.

When you pray for others, be comforted knowing Christ is praying for you (see Romans 8:33-34).

When you don't know what to say, trust him to speak on your behalf (see Romans 8:26).

When you fail to follow through, remember his grace covers you (see 2 Corinthians 12:8-9).

Pray right away—bringing every need and burden to the cross—and know that God hears every word you say. He is already working.

Word before World

It's not the thought that counts;
it's the prayer that makes a difference.

Grow in Grace

The next time someone asks for prayer, pray right away—
whether it's in your heart, out loud, or with a written note.

19

GOD IS NOT HIDING

O LORD, how manifold are your works!
In wisdom have you made them all.

PSALM 104:24

'Ve often prayed, "Lord, I want to see you," as if God were hiding from me. I've begged, "Lord, I want to hear you," as if he has gone silent or his Word has become void.

The truth is, God never stops speaking through Scripture; we simply become too busy to be still, look around us, listen, and linger in his presence (see Romans 1:20; Hebrews 4:12).

The glory of God spans the heavens above—brushstrokes of feathered clouds, a glowing crescent moon, a rainbow stretching across the sky after a storm, and shooting stars that beckon us to worship (see Psalm 19:1-2). Trees clap joyfully, swaying in the breeze, sending their roots down into the soil as they praise God, who planted them (see Isaiah 55:12).

Everywhere we look, God's creation reminds us of truths about his character. The flowers we buy at the grocery store to admire and set in vases on the kitchen counter inevitably fade, reminding us that life is fleeting but God's Word endures forever (see 1 Peter 1:24-25). The beams of light radiating from the sun expose darkness, just as the light of the gospel reveals the darkness of sin in our hearts (see Ephesians 5:13). Trees stretch out their limbs to receive light from the sun and produce fruit, but they must also stay connected to the plant for nutrients. In the same way, we must remain attached to Jesus, the true Vine, our source of life (see John 15:1-11).

God, the Creator of the universe, reflects his glory through his creation (see Psalm 8:1-4). His thumbprint is stamped on this world and in the marrow of our own bones. He is speaking, he is moving, he is with us. It's not that God has gone silent or hidden; it's that we have become blinded and our ears have become clogged with the noise of life.

The life-giving words of Scripture are a defibrillator, shocking the lifeless soul out of its slumber. They pulse new life into stone-cold hearts (see Psalm 119:25).

If we truly want to see God and hear God, we have to know him first through the Word, where he has revealed himself. As you go about your day, open your eyes to God's character as he reveals himself through his creation and through his Word.

Word before World

God has revealed himself to us through his Word
and through the world he has made.

Grow in Grace

Take a walk outside, if you can, or sit next to a window.
What details of God's creation do you notice?
How does beholding God's glory in
creation remind you of his character?

PRAISE GOD
WITH YOUR
TINY
HALLELUJAHS

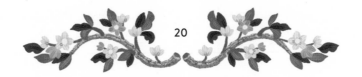

20

HIS PLANS > MY PLANS

As the rain and the snow come down from heaven and do not return there
but water the earth, making it bring forth and sprout, giving seed to
the sower and bread to the eater, so shall my word be that goes out from
my mouth; it shall not return to me empty, but it shall accomplish that
which I purpose, and shall succeed in the thing for which I sent it.

ISAIAH 55:10-11

My plans are better than yours,"
I carelessly say to the Lord.
"I've scheduled my days,
I'm set in my ways.
Please, won't you get on board?"

I balk, I complain, I scratch out.
I pencil in what I imagine should be.
My eyes see a glimpse
Of each problem—I wince
At the bewildering road before me.

What I dream—it tends to unravel
Like a loose thread unfastening a seam.
Then I throw a fit
And threaten to quit.
Oh Lord, can my plans be redeemed?

"My plans are better than yours,"
The Lord gently responds to me.
"I know what's to come—

My words can't be undone.
It's my way that will set you free."

I finally surrender my pen
To the one who created the ink.
For he sees it all—
And to him I call
When I'm teetering close to the brink.

For as the rain and the snow
Always fall from the sky,
Helping farmers to sow,
Lovely flowers to grow,
God will always be my supply.

My plans still change on a whim,
Even when I don't want them to.
But I trust my God's ways
To lead me each day,
For he has always seen me through.

Word before World

God's eternity-focused will and ways are better
than our short-sighted whims and plans.

Grow in Grace

Pull out your calendar. What are your biggest plans for the day
and week ahead? What would it look like to hold these plans
loosely and surrender them to the Father, who loves you?

21

SOUL FRUIT

I planted, Apollos watered, but God gave the growth.
So neither he who plants nor he who waters is
anything, but only God who gives the growth.

1 CORINTHIANS 3:6-7

Tiny seeds speckle the palms of my hands. A gust of wind could blow them away, so I hold them close as I poke holes into the freshly laid soil, drop them in place, and cover them with dirt.

Every year I find myself in the same predicament: anxious to plant these little seeds. It's not the planting that worries me; it's the waiting, the hoping, the day-by-day checking to see if they'll sprout.

What if this is the year they don't grow? What if snails sneak in overnight and eat the baby sprouts, like they did last year? What if I get too busy and forget to water each morning, and the sun scorches the flowers beyond recovery?

Though part of me rejoices when planting day finally arrives, I'm still a skeptic at heart, doubting God's ability to grow good fruit from such small, unimpressive seeds. Gardening is an act of pure faith. We dig, sow, water, weed, prune, and tend without being able to see the results at first—just clinging to the hope that we will one day enjoy the benefits of our labor.

When it comes to tending gardens and our souls, we tend to focus on growth and fruit. But what if it's not just about visible changes but about what's happening in the soil of our hearts?

Every year, my small seeds remind me that God uses both ordinary and monumental circumstances to mold, shape, teach, and grow us (see 2 Corinthians 3:18). Instead of focusing only on the fruit, we must start with gratitude for the gift of small beginnings and trust the growth to God (see 1 Corinthians 3:8-9).

Our lives are filled with opportunities to sow truth, such as speaking an encouraging word to a friend at just the right moment or sharing our faith with the person seated next to us on an airplane, or hugging the child who needs a reminder they are unconditionally loved (see Galatians 6:7-9; Ephesians 4:15, 29). The hours of our lives are filled with sowing moments and opportunities to grow in our faith as we trust God, the Gardener, to bring fruit in his perfect time.

As we root our faith firmly in the Word of God, God produces soul fruit within us. With our hope set on Jesus, we plant seeds in the soil of our own hearts and in the hearts of others, even though we don't know what fruit will come, if any at all (see Hebrews 6:19).

We press on, poking holes in the dirt and planting seeds, because even if nothing grows from the seeds we plant, we know that God is growing us all the while—teaching us to trust him, love him, and rely on him as he grows fruit in his own perfect time.

Word before World
God, the Gardener, produces soul fruit in our lives
as we plant seeds of obedience to his commands.

Grow in Grace
Think of someone you admire whose life demonstrates
good fruit for the Kingdom. Talk to them about their
journey of growth and how the master Gardener
has worked in their life over the years.

22

BLESSED

Blessed be the God and Father of our Lord Jesus Christ,
who has blessed us in Christ with every
spiritual blessing in the heavenly places.

EPHESIANS 1:3

In modern-day culture, the true meaning of the word *blessed* has been hijacked. Many people define it as having worldly success, good health, and abundant riches.

But the more I read Scripture, the more I realize that the meaning of blessing is countercultural—and so much deeper than the world's definition. Here are a few examples of types of people the Bible describes who are truly blessed: those who know Christ, those who are called according to his purpose, those who believe his Word, those whose sins are forgiven, those who live for the Kingdom of God, and those who suffer for Christ (see Matthew 16:16-17; Romans 8:28; Luke 11:28; Psalm 32:1; Matthew 6:33; Luke 6:22). It has made me wonder . . .

Is the blessing of God only the food on the table, or is it also the dry ground beneath the farmer's feet that makes him drop to his knees, earnestly praying for rain to soak the soil?

Is it only when your business grows and surpasses milestones, or is it also when you have to make the painful decision to close shop and follow God's leading down a new path?

Is it only when the pews of a church are packed on a Sunday, or is it also when the church meets secretly in a home, knowing persecution is right outside the door?

Is it only when health is vibrant and you're in the best shape of your life, or is it also found when you're enduring chemo and a stranger drops by your hospital room to pray with you?

Perhaps the blessing of God is both/and—the food on the table and the barren soil, the healthy checkup and the news that upends your plans. Maybe what is truly a blessing from the Lord doesn't look like abundance or ease but suffering and hardship that drives you to your knees.

The greatest blessing to ever reach our doorstep came through an infant, the Son of God, whose arrival did not appear to human eyes to be blessed. Thirty-three years later, Jesus suffered an excruciating death. The very hands that formed the world were nailed to a cross as his blood, which had the power to save, trickled to the ground. From death came God's best blessing.

Blessings aren't found only in good health, success, or achievement. It isn't experienced when you fit into a certain clothing size, gain a new relationship, or buy your dream home. No, true blessing is found when we are merciful to others, when we hunger and thirst for righteousness, when we strive for peace, when we are persecuted because of Jesus, and when we are pure in heart and poor in spirit (see Matthew 5:1-12). When we conform our lives to Christ, we enjoy eternal blessings found *only* in him (Romans 12:1-2).

When we are tempted to limit God's blessings to having our prayers answered in the way we desire, we'd be wise to remember his definition of blessing. It is often in the face of suffering we know Christ more and learn what it truly means to be blessed.

Word before World
In Christ, you are blessed beyond measure—
even if those blessings don't look
the way you imagine or expect.

Grow in Grace
Think of a time you limited God's definition of
what it means to be blessed. With the help of hindsight,
were you able to see how God brought blessings that
went beyond what you hoped for in the moment?

23

I LOVE YOU, LORD

I love you, O LORD, my strength.

PSALM 18:1

How often do you stop and tell God you love him? As you go through your day—running errands, sweeping crumbs, spending time with family, coworkers, and friends—does a deep love for God flavor your speech and fill your heart with joy?

I tell my children quite often that I love them. As they pretend to be superheroes or tell me a silly story, my heart brims with emotion and I can't help but tell them right away they are loved and cherished. I tell my husband I love him each time we part, even at the end of a quick call. It hit me recently: Do I do this for God, my Maker, my King, my Sustainer? Do I stop to tell him I love him, enjoy him, and delight in him?

So I've started making it a practice to tell God I love him as I go through my day. Instead of reserving adoration for when I'm at church or reading my Bible, I praise him as I go—both out loud and in my heart.

When you take a bite of your favorite meal, your mouth exploding with delight at the flavors God has made, tell him you love him.

When you go on an evening walk, the breeze tickling your skin and the glow of the setting sun contrasting the shadows of the trees, tell God you love him.

When you sit in the car for yet another commute or car pool line, tell God you love him.

When you are waiting for news from the doctor's office, tell God you love him.

When you laugh so hard you cry as you enjoy the company of good friends, tell God you love him.

When you listen to a sermon and the Holy Spirit stirs your heart to repentance and obedience, tell God you love him.

There is no time, no circumstance, no moment when love for God should not fuel our affections (see Matthew 22:37-39). Even when we walk through hardship, we can proclaim with our souls and our lips that we love the Lord. And when life is flourishing with joy-filled moments, we can proclaim again that his love endures forever.

It is not our love for God that draws us to him; rather, it's his love that drew us first (see 1 John 4:19). So tell God you love him today. Remind your soul of his goodness (see Psalm 136). Talk to him as you would talk to a friend. Pray in the easy moments as well as the hard moments.

Even when we falter and forget God, his love for us never fails (see Jeremiah 31:3; 1 Corinthians 13:8). Receive God's unfathomable grace. Marvel in his kindness toward you. Treasure the reality that you are fiercely loved by the same God who made the universe! May it become a reflex to dwell richly in God's love (see Ephesians 3:17-19; 1 John 4:16), to tell him we love him, and to praise him for his lovingkindness—both out loud with our lips and deep within our hearts.

Word before World

The steadfast love of the Lord never diminishes or dwindles. In response to this remarkable love, our hearts can overflow with praise and love for God.

Grow in Grace

Begin your day by telling God you love him. As you fill your
heart with adoration, it will become second nature for you
to express your love for God throughout the day.

24

TEARS OF MERCY

You have kept count of my tossings;
put my tears in your bottle. Are they not in your book?

PSALM 56:8

The tension I've been carrying squeezes the muscles in my shoulders, causing a throbbing headache. As I drive down the road with the kids in the back of the car, I'm lost in a myriad of thoughts—*What am I going to make for dinner tonight? How much longer till bedtime? Why is this season so hard?*—when my oldest shouts excitedly from the back seat, breaking my ruminations.

"Mom! Did you know butterflies drink turtle tears?" he asks in amazement.

All day I've been on the brink of crying. My husband has been traveling more frequently for work, and the stress of caring for three children while also working feels like a load of bricks I'm constantly carrying. Instead of letting the tears flow, I bottle them up in an attempt to keep them out of sight, deep in the recesses of my heart. I feel their persistent presence, but I ignore their need to be acknowledged.

"No, buddy, I've never heard that," I say, tucking this odd little fact into my mind and turning left onto our street.

Later that evening, after the kids are in bed and the last dirty dishes are loaded, I grab my laptop and do a quick internet search. To my surprise, there is a whole sermon hidden in this little fact my son has shared.

I learn that deep in the recesses of the Amazon rainforest, butterflies drink turtle tears for essential sodium and minerals. In turn, the turtles get their eyes cleaned.[1] Which begs the question: Why are turtles crying in the first place? Researchers note that turtles "cry" to moisten their eyes and clean them from dirt.[2] As I consider the tender way God cares for his creation, my eyes begin to burn with my own salty, bottled-up tears. If God provides for butterflies in the Amazon rainforest through the tears of turtles, how much more must he provide relief, healing, and hope for my own tears, even the ones I try to suppress and hide?

I've always found great comfort in King David's honest words in Psalm 56. Deep in the recesses of Gath, when he was being pursued by the Philistines, he penned a plea for mercy. Even as he cried for rescue, David found comfort in God's Word and his ever-present help. He clung to the promise that God saw his fear, weariness, and grief. He believed God wouldn't waste a single one of his tears; rather, he'd tenderly collect them in a bottle (see Psalm 56:8).

Just think—God, the Creator of the universe, not only provides for butterflies' needs through the tears of turtles, but he also notices every tear that falls from our eyes, including the ones we bottle up inside that need to fall. He is not unaware of our afflictions or aloof to them; instead, he draws near in the midst of them (see Psalm 34:18).

I finally give space to release the tears I'd been suppressing all day, knowing the Lord gives me strength for each day (see Deuteronomy 33:25). Someday when he comes to dwell with us forever in the new heavens and new earth, he will wipe away every tear, eradicate every fear, loosen every knotted shoulder, and unfurrow every brow (see Revelation 21:4). The old will pass away and the new will come, never to be undone.

Until then, we cry out to him for help, healing, and wholeness, because our tears are not spilled in vain—they are reminders of our reliance on our Maker.

Word before World

God notices every tear that falls and
draws near in your brokenness.

Grow in Grace

Take note of what makes you cry
(or makes you feel like you *need* to cry).
Instead of suppressing your tears, let them fall
before the Lord, and surrender your heartache to him.

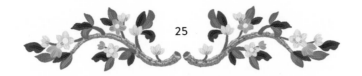

25

KNOW THAT YOU KNOW

Be merciful to those who doubt.

JUDE 22, NIV

'm no stranger to doubt. I used to believe having doubts meant my faith was mediocre and I was an inferior Christian. This belief pushed me away from God rather than toward him. Instead of seeking help beyond myself, I looked for help within, and when I did not find rescue, I spiraled into a black hole of skepticism.

On one of Jesus' journeys, he encountered a father and his demon-possessed son (see Mark 9:17-29). The father, desperate to see his child healed, brought him to Jesus after the disciples were unable to cast the demonic spirit out of him. When Jesus asked the father how long this had been happening, the father said he'd been suffering since childhood (verse 21).

"If you can do anything, have compassion on us and help us," the father begged Jesus (verse 22).

Do you see those three words exposing the father's frail belief? *If you can.*

This suffering father came before Jesus with doubt and belief at war in his heart. He could have given in to unbelief and sunk deeper into despair as he watched his son convulse and foam at the mouth. Yet even as he dragged the heavy weight of his doubt, he still came to Christ.

"'If you can'! All things are possible for one who believes," Jesus responded.

"I believe; help my unbelief!" the father confessed (verses 23-24).

At that moment, Jesus rebuked the evil spirit, and the convulsing in his muscles ceased. Even in the father's battle with unbelief, his faith was strengthened by the miracle of mercy.

As we walk on this earth in fallen bodies, we will struggle with unbelief and wrestle with doubt. When our minds are entrenched in unrelenting worry and feelings of hopelessness, we have a choice to make: Will we hold on tightly to our despair or turn our eyes on Jesus?

My pawpaw would often ask the question "Do you know that you know?" In other words, when you're faced with a tough decision or you're wrestling with doubt, do you know deep down what is true about God and the gospel?

When disbelief rages within, we can call these truths to mind:

I know that I know the Bible is God's living and active Word
(see Hebrews 4:12).
I know that I know the gospel transforms our hearts
(see 2 Corinthians 5:17).
I know that I know hope is found only in Jesus (see Hebrews 6:19-20).
I know that I know God uses my doubts to strengthen my faith in him
(see Matthew 14:31-33).

Doubts do not define us, but they can certainly refine us. When doubts lead us to the Word rather than away from it, they become the means to a stronger, deeper, fuller faith.

So turn your heart toward God, who is not afraid of your doubts. When your heart struggles to believe, confess your unbelief to the Lord. As Hebrews 4:16 reminds us, he can—and will—supply grace and mercy to help you in your time of need.

Word before World
Trusting God isn't something we do by feeling;
it's something we do by knowing.

Grow in Grace
List some of the doubts troubling your soul lately.
Rather than running from them, acknowledge them,
bring them to Christ, and humbly pray,
"I believe; help my unbelief!"

26

SOUL KEEPER

Only take care, and keep your soul diligently, lest you forget
the things that your eyes have seen, and lest they depart from
your heart all the days of your life. Make them known
to your children and your children's children.

DEUTERONOMY 4:9

I'm standing on the playground pushing my four-year-old on a swing when my friend and I start talking about our chronological Bible reading. "I get so frustrated with the Israelites!" she says. "One minute they're praising God, and the next they're complaining!"

Every time I read the Old Testament, I feel the same frustration—not only with the Israelites, but also with myself. Another friend of mine, Hilary, describes the forgetfulness of our souls as "Israelitis," a recurring condition I suffer from. My guess is that you've suffered from a bout of Israelitis at some point too.

After the Israelites' miraculous deliverance from slavery in Egypt, God appeared to Moses on Mount Sinai. The morning after one of Moses' hikes up the mountain, the Israelites witnessed bolts of lightning radiating from the cloud that covered the mountain (see Exodus 19:16-19). The mountain literally trembled at the presence of God.

In his holiness and kindness, the Lord warned the people not to come near the mountain or they would die (verses 21-22). You'd think this majestic sight, coupled with God's gracious protection, would be seared into their minds! Yet once again, the Israelites forgot the holiness of God and their promise of obedience to him.

During another of Moses' treks up the mountain, the Israelites got antsy waiting for Moses to come back down. Racked with impatience and afraid that something had happened to their leader, the Israelites approached Moses' brother, Aaron, and demanded that he make them a god to worship. Without delay or argument, Aaron gathered the people's gold, melted it in a fire, and formed a golden calf. To make matters worse, the Israelites credited their deliverance from Egyptian slavery to this human-made golden calf (see Exodus 32:4)!

Their audacity makes my jaw drop and my anger boil. How could the Israelites turn their backs on God after all he'd done for them? They had witnessed with their own eyes the Red Sea split in two! They had walked on dry ground between walls of water. They had watched Mount Sinai tremble before them, smoking with fire. But then they forgot—poof!—as if all this evidence of God's power had vanished from their minds.

In Deuteronomy, Moses recounts the many years and countless ways God led the Israelites out of slavery and through the wilderness to the Promised Land, providing for them every step of the way. He reminds them to remember, recite, and rehearse God's Word in their hearts so they can keep their souls grounded in truth (see Deuteronomy 4:9).

Thousands of years later, we still struggle with forgetfulness, just as the Israelites did. The only cure for "Israelitis" is to be soul keepers, kept by God as we diligently obey his commands. As Solomon reminds us, each of us must faithfully keep our heart "with all vigilance, for from it flow the springs of life" (Proverbs 4:23).

There will inevitably be times we forget what God has said and who he is. But when we return to God in repentance and faith, we will find grace and forgiveness—again and again.

Word before World

We can fight soul forgetfulness by reminding ourselves
of the gospel of Jesus Christ over and over again.

Grow in Grace

If you're suffering from a case of "Israelitis,"
confess your forgetfulness to God and turn away from
any idols you've erected. God will keep your soul as
you keep your eyes on him (see 1 Peter 1:5).

27

BURNED BLACK BEANS

He put a new song in my mouth, a song of praise to our God.
Many will see and fear, and put their trust in the LORD.

PSALM 40:3

urned black beans once made me break down into a puddle of tears. It wasn't just the burning of the beans that made me fall apart; it was the feeling of utter failure—like I was dropping all the plates I was trying to juggle and they were crashing at my feet in a thousand pieces.

Have you ever felt this way? When life seems out of control, one small mishap quickly becomes monumental. Case in point: burned black beans. The charred dinner wasn't really the source of my problem; rather, it exposed my inner struggle to let go of my plans and trust God's guidance and provision.

As I scraped the beans into the trash and ran hot, soapy water over the pan, the Lord showed me that I am not meant to carry the weight of the world on my shoulders.

I was reminded that day that I am limited, finite. We all are. Our strength and resolve go only so far until we become depleted. A tipping point inevitably comes, forcing us to wave our white flag and accept our limitations. It is only when we rely on Christ rather than ourselves that we experience his miraculous strength (see 2 Corinthians 12:9-10).

In the Kingdom of God, weakness is the entry point to experiencing

Christ's power. Jesus never told us life would be easy, our tasks would be effortless, or our calling would come naturally. Instead, he told us:

* He will be with us always as we proclaim the gospel (see Matthew 28:19-20).
* God will provide for all our needs through Christ (see Philippians 4:19).
* He will be our peace (see Ephesians 2:14).
* There's no need to fear because he is always near (see Isaiah 41:10).
* All God's promises find their yes in Jesus (see 2 Corinthians 1:20).

Black beans may still get burned, but they don't have to bury our hope in Jesus. When a small problem becomes a mountain in our lives, it's time to bow our pride before the Lord and receive his peace, strength, and refreshment (see James 4:10; 1 Peter 5:6-7). He is God; we are not. And that's a good thing.

That means we can set aside the plates we're juggling in an attempt to keep the world spinning. Christ carried the weight of the world in the form of a cross so we don't have to carry it ourselves (as if we could!). We are limited and weak, but he is strong and faithful.

Fortified by that truth, we can face small problems like burned dinner— not with a song of sorrow, but with a song of praise to God, who carries us all our days.

Word before World
Our limitations point us to God, who is faithful to provide for
our needs and able to sustain us through every setback.

Grow in Grace
Think of a time when something small became
monumental. How did you respond? How can you turn to
Christ in moments when life feels overwhelming?

28

TURN *WHY* INTO WORSHIP

He knows the way that I take;
when he has tried me, I shall come out as gold.

JOB 23:10

I will never understand why one womb can bear a quiver of children while another womb quivers with grief after yet another miscarriage.

I will never understand why one person is born into a family with two loving parents and another is abandoned at birth or abused in childhood.

I will never understand why cancer ravages one body while another lives into triple digits.

I will never understand how someone who loves Jesus can inflict pain on a fellow brother or sister in Christ.

I will never understand why some believers have access to countless Bibles while others face the possibility of death just for holding a page from God's Word.

The list could go on with all the things I will never fully make sense of while I inhabit this body and navigate life's questions with a limited mind. You likely have your own lengthy "I will never understand" list based on trials you've faced, worries you've wrestled with, and suffering you've endured and witnessed.

Jesus never promised we would understand everything on this side of heaven. The question is, will we be consumed by what we don't understand or will we allow what we know about God from his Word to form our response to life's sufferings?

One of the oldest recorded books of the Bible—Job—wrestles with the problem of pain and suffering. Though Job was a righteous man, God allowed Satan to sift him until he was pulverized by pain (see Job 1:6-12). In a matter of days, Job lost his wealth, his estate, his family, and his health.

His once fortunate life was reduced to ashes, burned by the fire of affliction and scattered by the wind of questioning. The bulk of the book of Job records back-and-forth conversations with his friends as they wrestle to understand why all this happened to righteous Job.

The book does not end with a detailed explanation of God's answers to their questions. Rather, it ends with an astonishing display of God's power—and humbling reminders that God can do anything.

The book of Job reveals to us that it is not wrong to ask why when we suffer (see Job 1:8; 7:20; see also Habakkuk 1:3). When we come to God with everything we don't understand, our Maker ministers to us and sustains us as we navigate life's hardest questions. He blows his winds of mercy through our forlorn souls and awakens us to his glory and grace.

For now, we wait, we wonder, and we wrestle. And though we may not understand, we can proclaim with Job: "I know that my Redeemer lives, and at the last he will stand upon the earth" (Job 19:25). When we don't understand the *why*, we can cling to the *who*.

Word before World

We will never fully understand the answers to all our questions, but we can face suffering with our eyes on Jesus, who has all understanding and power.

Grow in Grace

Acknowledging the things we will never understand leads us
to deeper worship of and surrender to our omniscient God.
Bring your whys to God, and let him turn them into worship.

29

TINY HALLELUJAHS

Give thanks to the LORD, for he is good,
for his steadfast love endures forever.

PSALM 136:1

What are you thankful for today? Depending on your current circumstances, you might have a long list at the tip of your tongue, or you might remain close-lipped, with nothing coming to mind.

There are days I'm bursting at the seams with gratitude. My eyes are wide open, and I spot good gifts from God all over the place (see James 1:17). On those days, praise flows from my heart naturally and freely. But if I'm being honest, my heart often suffers from a spiritual drought of thanksgiving. On those spiritually dry days, I need to harness the power of praising God with my tiny hallelujahs.

Psalm 136, a psalm of thanksgiving, recounts God's steadfast love through every moment of Israel's deliverance from Egypt. This psalm has a rhythmic framework, repeatedly calling God's people to give thanks to him, "for his steadfast love endures forever." The psalmist declares God's goodness as evidenced in the creation of the world (verses 4–9). He then fast-forwards to a step-by-step description of Israel's miraculous deliverance from slavery.

Like a beautiful melody, the psalm poetically highlights countless ways God revealed his faithfulness to his people, echoing the refrain "his steadfast love endures forever."

Each verse of Psalm 136 is like a tiny hallelujah, beautifully adding up to a mountain of praise. If God's people began reciting the psalm with ungrateful hearts, by the end, their dry hearts would have been well watered as they remembered God's faithfulness in every step of their journey.

Some of the examples of God's faithfulness feel unexpected. God didn't rescue his people from the Red Sea altogether; instead, he divided it and directed his people to pass *through* it (see verse 13) . He didn't take his people out of the wilderness; rather, he led his people through it (see verse 16). Yet God was with them, leading them and guiding them through each challenge. All these markers from the past remind us to search for God's fingerprints on every page of our own stories. God is *always* at work, even when we are blinded by ingratitude or shortsighted from worry.

If it's hard for you to find big feelings of gratitude today, praise God with your tiny hallelujahs. Resolve to give thanks, even when you don't feel like it. Each small act of thanksgiving will redirect your gaze to him and add up to a huge mountain that cannot be clouded by a heap of complaints.

Word before World

Tiny hallelujahs change our hearts and
open our eyes to God's fingerprints in our lives.

Grow in Grace

Make a gratitude list titled "My Tiny Hallelujahs" and
place it somewhere you will see it often. Continue to add to it,
even in moments when gratitude might not be your first response.
The more you look for God's hand at work, the more your eyes
will see God's faithfulness woven throughout your days.

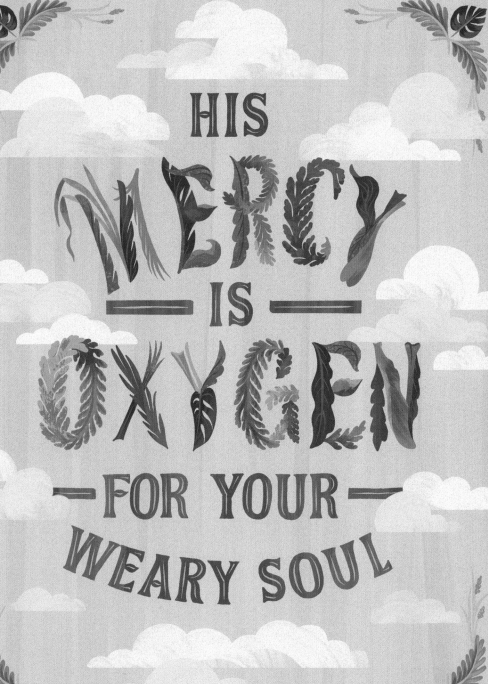

HIS
MERCY
— IS —
OXYGEN
— FOR YOUR —
WEARY SOUL

30

BRIGHT HOPE FOR TOMORROW

*May the God of hope fill you with all joy
and peace in believing, so that by the power
of the Holy Spirit you may abound in hope.*

ROMANS 15:13

Once a year, I find myself in a hospital waiting room for my thyroid ultrasound. I normally dread this day—the time it takes, the discomfort of having a probe pushed against my throat, the *What if they find something this time?* fear that pricks at my peace.

But although I feel trepidation about this appointment, I've come to see it as a yearly gift of remembrance, where I am faced with my mortality and the reality that for all who follow Christ, the best is yet to come (see Revelation 22:1-4).

With this in mind, I rehearse these three truths to my heart as I lie on the uncomfortable bed, waiting to be prodded:

1. **Our days are numbered.** King David writes, "Your eyes saw my unformed substance; in your book were written, every one of them, the days that were formed for me, when as yet there was none of them" (Psalm 139:16). We don't know if we will live another day or another half a century, and this should compel us to live each day with a heart of wisdom (see Psalm 90:12). Numbering our days is

not our natural inclination; it's a discipline we learn from God as we live out his Word (see Ephesians 5:15-17). Life on earth is brief—like the breath we exhale on a cold day that is here for a moment and disappears the next (see James 4:14-15). Live for what will last—the Kingdom and glory of God.

2. **We don't know what tomorrow holds, but we know the one who holds tomorrow.** Instead of boasting about our plans for the future, we make our boast in God, his goodness, and his grace in this present moment (2 Corinthians 12:6-10). He has given us the Holy Spirit to comfort and guide us into glory as we suffer with Christ (see John 14:26).

3. **We are finite human beings, held by our infinite and loving Father.** Though we face hardship and though our bodies break down and fall apart, he holds us together (see Isaiah 41:10). His Word and his eternal promises are steady and true, and his enduring love for us cannot be taken, broken, or shaken (see Romans 8:37-39).

So I'll continue to hold these yearly reminders as gifts, knowing that even though life is fragile and fleeting, God is forever faithful. He holds us in the palm of his hands, and his purposes are always for our good and his glory (see John 10:27-30; Romans 8:28).

When something reminds you of the brevity of life and the reality of eternity, don't turn away in denial. Instead, turn toward God in humility as you face the trial before you with his grace. No suffering we go through catches God off guard.

As the beloved hymn, "Great Is Thy Faithfulness" proclaims, God gives us not only "strength for today" but also "bright hope for tomorrow."

Word before World

We don't know what we will face today,
tomorrow, or in the weeks ahead.
But we can endure whatever comes because
the God of hope will fill us with joy and peace.

Grow in Grace

What reminders of your mortality
have you gotten lately?
Ask the Lord to teach you that
each day is a gift so you can live it with
a heart of wisdom (see Psalm 90:12).

31

GRIN AND LET GOD BEAR IT

Blessed be the Lord, who daily bears us up;
God is our salvation.

PSALM 68:19

Have you ever been in a season where margin feels minimal, responsibilities are burdensome, and any small shift in your daily schedule leads to a giant headache? Maybe you're in a low-margin season right now, dog-paddling to keep your head above water. Perhaps you expected this season to be filled to the brim and tried to prepare for it, bracing for the onslaught of stress, but now you're realizing that even careful preparation won't make this less grueling to walk through.

I'm in one of those seasons myself right now. I knew this time would be jam-packed, so I planned, prepped, and made adjustments, hoping to alleviate stress. In spite of all my efforts, however, each day is still exhausting, draining, and at times discouraging. I would like this season to be over *yesterday*, but our family still has to face weeks of shifting schedules, mounting pressures, and a disrupted rhythm.

In times like these, I see how quick I am to try to build my hope on consistency, comfort, and control. When God brings an earthquake to my unrealistic expectations and faulty foundations, the cracks in my faith are exposed. That's when I have the opportunity to rebuild on Christ alone.

When my husband, Greg, and I were planning for this season, we tossed the phrase "I guess we'll have to grin and bear it" at each other, trying to assuage our weary hearts. As the days and weeks have progressed and our shifty foundation has been tested, I no longer believe we have to grin and bear it. Rather, we get to grin and let *God* bear it.

Psalm 68 records King David's song of praise to God, who delivers his people, leads them, and provides for them. Rather than looking inward to find help and security, David looked upward for rescue. In verse 19, he praised God, saying, "Blessed be the Lord, who daily bears us up; God is our salvation." When life feels unbearable, God bears us up.

The Hebrew word for bear means to "carry a load."[1] As a compassionate father, God carries us through hardship, taking on the burdens that bear down on our hearts, and bringing us to a place of rest. He doesn't just bear us up once or twice; he mercifully carries us every moment of every day. Not only does God hold us in his capable arms, but he does so joyfully (see Isaiah 41:10; 46:4; Ephesians 1:3). Knowing we are not a burden to him, we can grin in the face of busyness and stress, confident of God's presence and provision (see Psalm 13:5-6; 126:3).

As you walk through stressful seasons, when you are stretched on all sides, you can bless the Lord, who bears you up. Instead of trying to endure on your own strength and grit, grin and let God bear it. He gives power and strength to his people (see Psalm 68:35), and that includes you and me.

Word before World
When you face a stressful season, you don't have to muster up
your own strength to make it through. You can trust God,
who will bear you up and sustain you each day.

Grow in Grace
What burdens are you carrying right now that you weren't created
to bear? Read Psalm 68:19, and insert your name in the verse.
Then hand over your burdens to our gracious, powerful God.

32

PRAISE LIKE CONFETTI

Pray without ceasing, give thanks in all circumstances;
for this is the will of God in Christ Jesus for you.

1 THESSALONIANS 5:17-18

Today as I was picking up around the house, I found myself running through a litany of complaints: *Why can't my house stay clean for one entire day without being torn apart? Am I the only one who struggles to get dinner on the table? Will I ever feel rested again?*

Maybe you've been there too. Some days we hoard complaints in our hearts, keeping tabs on everything that's going wrong around us. The more things go wrong, the more we try to white-knuckle our grip on control.

Ingratitude causes our vision of what truly matters to become hazy. I've had seasons when my eyes were fixed on the temporary problems before me and within me, and I struggled to be truly grateful.

If your heart is packed with problems, gripes, and grievances, you're certainly not alone. But we don't have to make our home here. When complaints preoccupy our minds, it's time to overhaul our ungrateful hearts and refresh our vision.

If you don't know where to start when it comes to renovating your heart, here are a few simple ideas:

1. **Diagnose the source of your ingratitude.** What's driving you to be ungrateful? What lie or false belief is clouding your vision and preventing you from seeing all that God has done and is doing? Instead of allowing ingratitude to consume your peace, name it, bring it to Jesus, and ask him to help you see his sovereignty and goodness over the course of your life (Philippians 4:6-7).

2. **Remember what God has done.** Open your Bible and read his Word. Remember how God provided manna for the Israelites as they wandered in the wilderness (see Exodus 16). Read about how God heard Hannah's prayer for a son and answered in his perfect timing (see 1 Samuel 1). Find out how Paul pleaded for God to remove his thorn in the flesh and how he came to delight in God's provision of strength (see 2 Corinthians 12:7-10). Read until your heart is cleared of the clutter of complaints—or at least until you can breathe a sigh of thanks (see Psalm 136:1). If God delivered the Israelites from their slavery (see Exodus 15:1-6), transformed Ruth's life (see Ruth 4:13-15), forgave David's transgressions (see Psalm 51), rescued Jonah from drowning and sustained his life in the belly of a big fish (see Jonah 1:12-17; 2), and saved Paul from a hell-bound life (see Acts 9:1-9), surely he won't pass you by. You aren't the exception to God's faithfulness.

3. **Thank God in advance for his provision and grace.** Rather than worrying about tomorrow, rehearsing all the things that could go wrong, or coveting all that's going right in someone else's life, thank God for all the ways he will show up with his faithfulness and provision, precisely when we need it (see Psalm 103:2; Philippians 4:19).

The gospel reminds us that there is nothing we can do to save ourselves from our sins but that Christ has made a way for salvation through his sinless life and perfect sacrifice. He carried the weight of our sin and ingratitude on his shoulders so we could have full, abundant life in him (see John 10:10). When our eyes are fixed on Jesus, not the problems before us, our grumblings turn into gratitude and our complaints turn into confetti-like praise, sprinkling joy, light, and life all around us.

Word before World
The gospel clears out the complaints in our hearts
so we can see Jesus more clearly and
give thanks for all he has done.

Grow in Grace
Write down the false beliefs or fears that drive you
toward ingratitude. Now apply the gospel to these.
What is proved true in Jesus' life, death, and resurrection?

WONDERSTRUCK

Bless the LORD, O my soul! O LORD my God,
you are very great! You are clothed with splendor and majesty,
covering yourself with light as with a garment.

PSALM 104:1-2

The moon was the biggest I'd ever seen. It hovered in the sky right down the street from us, so close that it seemed God had lassoed it and pulled it near the earth. My older son squealed in excitement and ran to retrieve the wobbly, gray telescope his pappy had given him, his younger brother trailing close behind.

Smack-dab in the middle of the cul-de-sac, he set up an observation station to admire the moon lighting the night. My little boy's palpable delight spread to my own heart as I watched him soak in God's glory reflected by the glowing moon, up close and personal.

✳ ✳ ✳

Wonderstruck: (1) an out-of-the-blue feeling of awe and wonder; (2) like being struck by lightning and surviving to tell the tale; (3) like a baby tasting buttercream-frosted cake for the first time when she's only had rice cereal before; (4) like truly seeing, with eyes wide open, the astonishing provision of God when you've previously slotted everyday miracles as ordinary happenstance (see Psalm 92:5).

* * *

I couldn't believe my eyes. I gazed in wonder at my computer screen, taking in the recently released images of the Cosmic Cliffs of the Carina Nebula, captured by NASA's James Webb Space Telescope.[1] My first thought was, *This can't be real.* My next thought was, *How great is our God!*

In these images of shimmering stars being born, it looked like glitter had been sprinkled across the night sky. I was literally starstruck.

We serve the same God who speaks and stars are born! What has taken humankind centuries to discover, God has been keeping in motion all along (see Genesis 1:1; Isaiah 40:26).

* * *

Anxiety often hits me hardest at night, when the sun goes down and the moon softly glows. I don't think I'm alone in this. It's in the darkness that our minds tend to fixate on all the things that could go wrong. We lie in bed, hearts racing, tossing and turning, praying for sleep while shadows cover the room.

In moments like these, we need a larger vision, a wider view of God's greatness. This is where Psalm 104 comes in, hushing our worried souls with reminders of God's infinite power. God, who "made the moon to mark the seasons," knows every thought in our minds, including the ones that wreak havoc on our hearts (see Psalm 104:19; 139:1-2). His glory spans the heavens, and his Word illuminates the paths before us, leading us from being worried to being wonderstruck (see Psalm 19:1; 119:105).

When we are lying in bed stricken by fear, stars are still being born above us. God is greater than our minds can comprehend, more powerful than we realize. A glimpse at the moon through a telescope or a careful study of images in the Carina Nebula doesn't even compare to the one who created the night sky. But in these moments, our view of the greatness of God is enlarged. He lassoes us and pulls us close—and we are wonder-struck.

Word before World
Awe enlarges our vision of God's greatness.

Grow in Grace
When was the last time you were wonderstruck
by God's greatness? If you can, go outside and look at
the stars (or look up NASA's images of stars online).
What strikes you about God's handiwork?

34

WHAT IF?

It is he who remembered us in our low estate,
for his steadfast love endures forever; and rescued us
from our foes, for his steadfast love endures forever.

PSALM 136:23-24

Almost every time something good happens to me, I find myself wondering, *What if something bad happens next?* Years ago, I walked through a series of health crises that came on the heels of a busy season of travel and overcommitment. After that experience, I began associating joyful moments with a sense of foreboding. I was convinced that the worst was on its way, and my brain hypothesized all the negative scenarios that could happen. In some twisted way, I convinced myself that if I could conjure up all the scenarios that might transpire, I could preemptively prepare for heartache and protect myself from pain.

Rather than protecting me, however, this destructive thought pattern became a roadblock to praising God and experiencing peace in Christ. Instead of giving thanks to God for answered prayer, victory over sin, and daily provision, I started second-guessing his character, believing he would snatch good gifts from me as quickly as they came.

At the core of our what-ifs is the false belief that God isn't good and that he isn't always good *to us*. When we allow what-ifs to dominate our thinking, our fears escalate, overshadowing the foundational truth that God is sovereign and is always at work, even in the midst of gut-wrenching heartache, chronic pain, and unexpected trouble.

The knowledge of God's sovereignty does not prevent us from walking through hardship, but it does offer us an anchoring hope in the storm (see

Hebrews 6:19). It's true that we live in a fallen world where bad things happen, and no amount of protection or preparation can shield us from experiencing the effects of sin. But it's also true that we have access to indescribable joy that transcends any and all heartache (see Psalm 16:11).

Instead of bracing for the bad that *could* happen, what if we joined the psalmist and gave thanks to the Lord for all the good he has done, is doing, and will continue to do (see Psalm 136)? What if, instead of anticipating everything that could go wrong, we chose to praise God for his faithfulness in the things we can see, as well as the things we can't see (see Hebrews 11:1)?

Praise is always possible. Giving thanks to God for what he has done, what he is doing, and what he will do moves us from asking "What if?" to being filled with assurance of his steadfast love. Whether we are dancing on a mountaintop or grieving in a valley, God's love holds us, heals us, and helps us endure with joy. In every place, in every season, God is good—and he is good to us.

Sister, there is no need to fear what could come today. God already knows. This moment is what we have, and at this moment we can experience joy as we fix our eyes on Jesus, who endured the cross "for the joy set before him" (Hebrews 12:2, NIV).

Eternal joy is ours in Jesus. Rather than spending your time worrying about what might or might not happen, embrace the ever-present help and hope you have in Christ. In all things, he is God, he is good, and his steadfast love endures forever.

Word before World
We do not need to fear what tomorrow holds;
rather, we can praise God for his faithfulness today.

Grow in Grace
Ask the Holy Spirit to lead you out of the land of what-if and into the love of the Lord, who remembers us and rescues us, all because of his steadfast love.

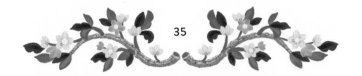

35

RUN THE RIGHT RACE

I press on toward the goal for the prize
of the upward call of God in Christ Jesus.

PHILIPPIANS 3:14

"I can't keep up, Lord. I feel like I am falling behind in everything," I scribble in my journal. "Even reading my Bible feels like another area where I am failing to keep up."

At the beginning of the year, I set out to read the entire Bible from start to finish. I'm woefully behind in my reading plan, inching along at a snail's pace. My house is a disaster, and the laundry is never fully done, no matter how hard I try. Add to that the other responsibilities and relationships I'm struggling to keep up with—work, marriage, motherhood, cooking, friendship, and more—and the long list of unfinished business rivals the Pan-American Highway.

"My unrealistic expectations make me feel exhausted and frustrated, Lord. I just can't keep up with this pace or finish this race I'm running. What am I to do?"

As the day progresses, I keep confessing the same words to the Lord: "I can't keep up." As I pray and ponder and plead for help, this question comes to mind: *What race are you running?* Deep down, I know the answer. I'm running a race for control over my life—and this is a race that can never be won.

Hebrews 12:1-2 says, "Since we are surrounded by so great a cloud of witnesses, let us also lay aside every weight and sin which clings so closely, and let us run with endurance the race that is set before us, looking to Jesus, the founder and perfecter of our faith." More often than not, we wear heavy weights around our necks—the weight of expectations, the weight of people-pleasing, the weight of perfection. These weights are not put on us by God. They do not make us more spiritual or holy; they only hold us back from walking in true gospel freedom.

When our eyes are fixed on what others are achieving or how much we can check off a to-do list, we enter a race we were never meant to run. But when our eyes are fixed on Jesus, we run the race he has set before us, unhindered by the burden of extra baggage. This race is not about winning or competing against others; rather, it's about glorifying God every step of the way as we follow his footsteps. The pressure to keep up is gone, because in Christ, we are set free from the need to prove our worth. We already have victory in the race that truly matters (see 1 Corinthians 15:57).

If you feel like you are falling behind and can't keep up, remember: you cannot fall behind when you are following Jesus. Run the race set before you with your eyes glued on your Savior. As you do, the heavy weights you've been carrying will fall to the wayside, and the pressures you've been facing will narrow to one thing: pressing on toward Jesus.

Word before World
You cannot fall behind when you are following Jesus.

Grow in Grace
What weights have you been hauling around
that Jesus never asked you to carry? Ask him to
help you lay aside those weights so you can run
the race before you in freedom, fullness, and joy.

36

SIMMER IN SCRIPTURE

His delight is in the law of the LORD,
and on his law he meditates day and night.

PSALM 1:2

If you want a recipe for a life of joy in Christ, you'll find it in the spiritual discipline of biblical meditation.

Each week when I meal plan, I check the weather to see if there are any chilly or rainy days ahead so I can plan my menu accordingly. If the forecast predicts a cold day, I can almost guarantee you'll find a pot of our favorite chicken tortilla soup or zuppa Toscana simmering on the stove.

A delicious, satisfying soup doesn't come together simply by pouring all the ingredients into a pot; the secret is to let it simmer. The longer the soup simmers, the more the flavors expand and mingle together. I'm convinced that most soups are even tastier the next day. Likewise, the more we simmer our souls in Scripture, letting it soak into our minds and transform our thoughts, the more we will enjoy the blessings of God's Word.

The psalmist explains that the "blessed" person is the one who delights in God's law and meditates on it day and night (Psalm 1:1-2). The Hebrew word for *meditate* can also be translated as "to muse, imagine."[1] The person who is happiest and most fulfilled thinks deeply about the Word of God, considering each word and savoring God's revelation to humans as the greatest treasure of all.

The art of biblical meditation does not simply involve a cursory reading of Scripture. Rather, it requires a slow, thoughtful simmer in the Word—like the process of cooking soup.

Here's a "recipe" for meditating on God's Word:

1. **Choose a verse or passage of Scripture to meditate on.** If you are new to biblical meditation, Psalms is a great starting place. (Consider Psalm 19, 23, 42, or 139.)

2. **Read the passage several times.** This will help you gain a fuller understanding of the context. Just as you'd read a new recipe several times to get the gist of how it will come together, we faithfully read God's Word in its greater context before we zoom in. Consistent Bible reading leads to deeper understanding.

3. **Think deeply about each line and each word.** This may seem odd at first if you're used to reading quickly. But as you slow down to digest the meaning of the words you're reading, connecting what's in your head to what you believe in your heart, you'll enjoy a richer grasp of God's promises. You can meditate on the meaning by reading the verse multiple times, with an emphasis on a different word each time.

4. **Use God's Word as a means for prayer and worship.** The psalms, specifically, add depth and flavor to one's prayer life. As you meditate on Scripture, you can use the living and active Word of God as a springboard for your own petitions, praises, and conversations with the Lord. This can look like praying the psalms just as they are written or using what you learn from them to form your own heartfelt prayers to the Lord.

The more you slow down your Bible reading and intentionally meditate on God's Word, the more you'll find that simmering in Scripture is not a burdensome task; it's a delight to the heart. Like a chef who gathers her ingredients, sets her stockpot on the stove, and patiently stirs her soup, soak your soul in God's life-giving Word. This is the key to a savor-worthy life in Christ.

Word before World

Simmering your soul in Scripture
is not a burdensome task;
it is the key to abundance and joy in Christ.

Grow in Grace

Pick a verse or passage of Scripture to
begin meditating on this week. Each day,
spend five to ten minutes pondering the passage,
letting God's Word simmer in your soul.

37

MICROWAVING GRACE

The steadfast love of the LORD never ceases; his mercies never come
to an end; they are new every morning; great is your faithfulness.

LAMENTATIONS 3:22-23

Most nights I go to bed anticipating the first hot cup of coffee I'll have in the morning. If you're not a coffee drinker, you might not understand this, but maybe you have another drink or treat you look forward to each day.

One particular morning, I woke up before dawn and headed to the kitchen to grab my much-anticipated first cup. At this time of day, I cannot be held accountable for what I do, because my brain is working at only about 30 percent. I eagerly poured my cup of caffeine and topped it off with a splash of vanilla creamer.

I lifted it to my mouth for the first sip and received a rude awakening. The coffee was *cold*! I wasn't met with the hot, fresh sip I was hoping for but an old, cold cup of coffee. No amount of creamer, whipped cream, or microwaving would help this pitiful brew. It certainly woke me up—just not in the way I'd anticipated! Somehow when I'd prepped our coffeepot the night before, I started it instead of setting it on the timer.

As I made a fresh pot of coffee, I remembered that God is a giver of fresh grace, not stale mercy or leftover hope. He does not give his children scraps or leftovers of his love. Instead, he lavishly pours fresh mercy on our needy hearts every day, filling our empty cups with exactly what we need.

As followers of Jesus, we should live in a way that shows those around us this refreshing truth: God's grace is real and abundant and can be found only in Christ. All too often, we put the world before the Word and our love for Jesus grows cold. When our priorities are out of place, we live according to the desires of our flesh rather than the power of the Holy Spirit (see Romans 8:6-10). But we don't have to live like God's grace is an old, cold cup of coffee—grumbling and complaining. We can joyfully soak in his mercies each day, like that first sip of piping hot coffee.

Even when our love for God grows stale, his grace is greater. He can warm our cold souls again through the power of his Word and the work of the Holy Spirit. On that morning when my lips were greeted with cold coffee, I started the pot again and refreshed my cup, sipping with a level of gratitude that wouldn't have been there had I not tasted the stale coffee.

However your soul is feeling today—cold, lukewarm, or piping hot—bring Jesus your empty cup and let him fill it with new morning mercies and fresh grace.

Word before World

God's mercies are new not only in the morning
but also in the afternoon and in the evening
(and in every hour between).

Grow in Grace

In the times when it feels like your love for
God has grown cold, read Psalm 119:97-104
and refresh your soul in God's Word.

38

BLOOMING IN WINTER

Behold, I am doing a new thing; now it springs forth,
do you not perceive it? I will make a way
in the wilderness and rivers in the desert.

ISAIAH 43:19

In the blistering heat of summer, I bought a Christmas cactus at a farmer's market, hoping to enjoy fiery red blooms when winter came. I researched optimal conditions for this plant and tried to replicate them in my home. But deep down, I was almost certain my little plant wouldn't survive my rookie gardening know-how.

When November came, I moved the fledgling plant to our sunroom, gave it a spritz of water, and left it there—out of sight, out of mind. In the winter, I avoid the sunroom altogether. It isn't heated, so even when sunlight filters in, it remains frigid.

One day, after the cactus had been left alone for quite some time, I opened the curtains and spotted a bloom that had grown when I wasn't paying attention.

As the days progressed, more tiny cherry-colored buds appeared and began to unfurl. Like icicles slowly melting, tears puddled in my eyes as I beheld this winter wonder. Even when the world looks barren and we are huddled indoors, God is still growing good things. He purposefully made this little cactus to bloom wildly in winter. So it is with our lives. He brings light and color to our gray world in places we least expect, and he brings hope when we aren't even looking.

You may be facing a season in your life when the ground seems fallow, blooms have retreated, and it feels impossible to believe that beauty could come from your brokenness. Or perhaps you are facing pressure at work, the weight of being a full-time caregiver, or the tragedy of loss, divorce, or a medical diagnosis, and all you can do right now is survive. You are longing for growth, for God to bring something beautiful out of the soil of your soul. Remember this: God is always at work beneath the surface, even if you can't see the evidence right now. He will bring good things to fruition in his perfect timing.

Isaiah 43:18-19 holds a beautiful promise from God to the Israelites, calling them to forget the past and behold the new things he would do. Isaiah prophesied these words to serve as a comfort to the people of Judah, who would soon endure a seventy-year exile in Babylon. No matter how dismal their circumstances, God would cup their chins and lift their eyes so they could behold the new ways he was working.

God calls us to do the same. Even when you can't see any blooms, growth is still happening. When life feels barren, trust the good work he is doing underground, and believe that one day you will feel the thrill of beholding a tiny unsuspecting bud in the soil of your soul.

Word before World
Even when we can't see the evidence,
God grows good things in the soil of our souls.

Grow in Grace
Think back on a season you've endured
that felt barren. Looking back, what growth can
you see, proving that God was working all along?

39

A FLASHLIGHT IN THE DARK

The light shines in the darkness,
and the darkness has not overcome it.

JOHN 1:5

No human is immune to suffering. The dark night descends on all of us at one point or another, an unwelcome guest that takes residence in our soul. When darkness seems to hide the face of God, our first natural inclination is to hide our face from others. We try to conceal the pain, disguise the fear, protect the wound.

I've walked through many of these dark nights myself, the most recent after having my third child. I hit a low spot a month and a half postpartum.

Weeping uncontrollably, with my hands covering my makeup-free, tearstained face, I sat on a metal chair in my doctor's office with a nurse consoling me, handing me tissues, and listening to my grief. She offered her own postpartum story as a shared bond.

Dr. B., a sister in Christ, came in and crouched down next to me so she could be at my eye level. Rather than towering above me, as most doctors do, she stooped low, touched my shoulder, and gave me both the hope of the gospel for my soul and the help of medicine for my body. I received her words of wisdom with clenched fists, wanting to shoo away the clouds of depression on my own, frustrated that I needed help in the first place.

I wasn't ready to receive it yet, but God was providing healing in his own, higher way (see Isaiah 55:8-9).

Back at home, friends showed up, one by one. They provided meals and went grocery shopping for me. They cleaned my fridge, handed me bowls of watermelon to snack on, prayed for me, allowed me to cry on their shoulders, and sent care packages in the mail when they were too far away to come in person. Texts saying, "I'm praying for you" were like beams of hope, flashlights in the darkness.

They understood. They cared. Their presence reminded me that God understands. He cares. And he provides—through his Word and his people.

During that season, it felt like an insurmountable task to even open my Bible. The pages seemed to be glued together, and the words jumbled in my mind when I tried to read them. Smiling felt impossible, healing seemed far off, and crocodile tears were the norm. And yet God prompted me to show my tearstained face to my friends, neighbors, and church family. He blew away the clouds that seemed to hide his face, showing me that the Son still shines, even when a storm blows in.

In this dark night of my soul, when sleep would not come and joy felt impossible, the Good Shepherd made me lie down, restored my soul, and invited me to rest in his unchanging grace (see Psalm 23). He offered me flashlights in the darkness that came in the form of the words, help, and presence of my family and friends. Their presence, along with the Scriptures I'd stored in my heart in the years prior, were lifelines for my soul.

The torrent of tears has dried up since then, but the memory of that time can never be erased. No matter what storm we weather, the sun always shines again. And no matter what dark night of the soul we endure, we know that God sees our face and hears our voice. Regardless of how bleak things look, he always shines a flashlight of gospel hope into the darkness.

Word before World

When we cannot see God's hand at work,
he provides flashlights in the dark through the
presence of his people and the promises of his Word.

Grow in Grace

Think back on a time when a dark night descended
on your soul and you couldn't see God at work.
How did he provide flashlights to remind you
of his power, protection, and presence?

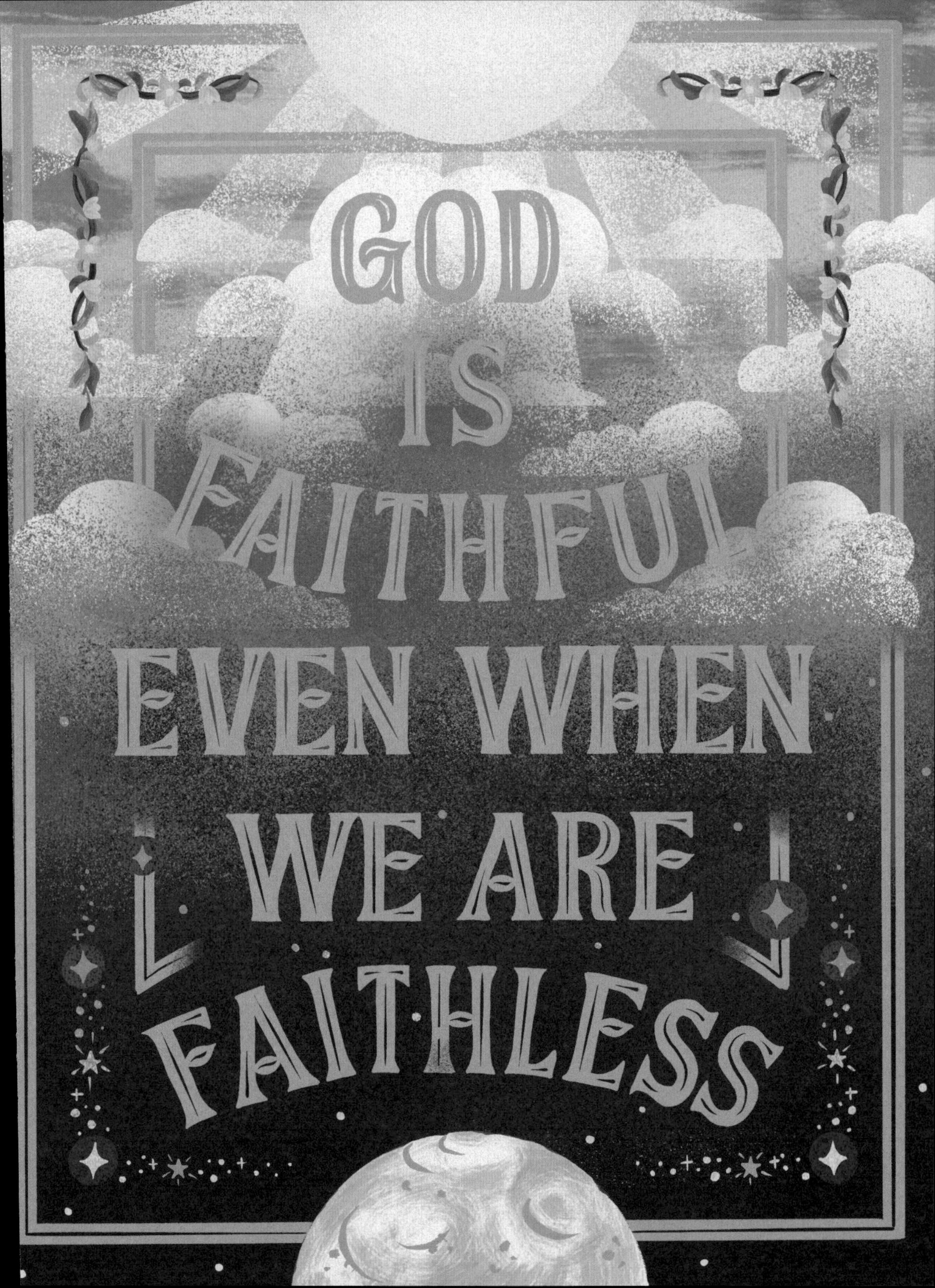
GOD
IS
FAITHFUL
EVEN WHEN
WE ARE
FAITHLESS

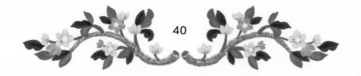

40

COME AS YOU ARE

Come now, let us reason together, says the LORD: though your sins are like scarlet,
they shall be as white as snow; though they are red like crimson, they shall become like wool.

ISAIAH 1:18

We're driving to church when I hear the words every parent dreads from the back seat: "Where are my shoes?"

Greg and I glance at each other, wide-eyed, as if to say, *Did you grab his shoes?* We quickly realize we have a choice: either we have to turn around and miss church or we stay the course without shoes.

It just so happens that the child who forgot his shoes is the one with the most tender heart. He is highly aware of those around him, and he feels emotions deeply (like his mom). I think about how I would feel going to church without shoes, and my heart aches for him. But I sense God reminding me that church is not about showing off our Sunday best; it's about showing up just as we are to worship our King.

After a quick front-seat chat with my husband, we break the news to our son that he will have to go to church without his shoes.

"But what if they don't let me in?" he asks, his eyes welling with tears.

"Buddy, Jesus loves you even when you have no shoes on," I assure his worried heart. "He welcomes you to come just as you are. The people at our church will do the same!"

By the time we arrive, the concern on his face has grown. I carry him inside with sock-clad feet, but not a soul notices—nor would they care if they did. Church isn't about presenting ourselves as all buttoned up, with stray hairs combed into place and problems shoved behind closed doors. We come just as we are, receiving the grace Jesus freely gives (see John 1:16). And we give grace to others, as freely as we have received ourselves (see Matthew 10:8).

We all have moments when we are forced to reckon with the reality that we don't have it all together, even if we pretend to. Either we can hide our problems and miss out on receiving the gift of God's grace or we can show up and receive the love of Christ. How many times do we miss out on the blessing of being truly seen by fellow Christians because we are consumed by the unrealistic expectation that we must have our act together?

Jesus calls us to come and receive the living water that always satisfies and never runs dry (see John 4:14). He welcomes with open arms all who carry heavy burdens, urging us to find rest in him (see Matthew 11:28-30). He calls sinners to come and be scrubbed clean from their sins (see Isaiah 1:18). He beckons the parched soul to drink and the hungry belly to feast at his table (see Isaiah 55:1-2).

That day, Jesus called my son to come to church without shoes on. I smile as I think about how I carried him into church with only his socks on, hoping he would experience the love, grace, and provision of God in a new and deeper way.

If you feel embarrassed or ashamed today, come and approach the throne of grace with your head held high, knowing your debt has been paid. Receive your Savior's help, and let him wrap his lavish love around you in your time of need—whether you've got your shoes on or not.

Word before World

Jesus loves you even in the moments when you don't have your act together.

Grow in Grace

What is holding you back from coming to Christ just as you are?
Lay aside your guilt, shame, and imperfection, and come boldly before
the throne of grace with confidence, knowing God has covered you,
welcomed you, and forgiven you in Christ.

41

WHEN I GROW UP

Grow in the grace and knowledge
of our Lord and Savior Jesus Christ.

2 PETER 3:18

One of the most common questions kids get asked is, "What do you want to be when you grow up?"

When I was little, my answer changed almost by the hour. Some days I wanted to be an artist, painting lavender lilacs like Mary Cassatt. Other days I dreamed of being a marine biologist (which wouldn't have worked out well since I have a slight fear of swimming in the ocean). At times I wanted to be an haute couture fashion designer, and other times I dreamed about being an elementary school teacher just so I could grade papers with a bright red pen.

Now, years later, I'm an adult and I do none of those things. God has shifted my path over and over again, and each time I find myself surprised by the twists and turns that somehow lead me to the exact place I'm supposed to be. I'm a grown-up by the world's definition, but I'm still in the process of growing in grace as I become more like Christ.

The truth is, we never finish growing up as believers, because we are always growing in Christ. We never arrive; we simply keep moving forward, coming to know him more and becoming more like him until we breathe our last.

Yet all too often, we put off living faithfully today, thinking obedience will be easier tomorrow when we are older and wiser. We tally a long list of spiritual hurdles and milestones we want to conquer when we "grow up," and we miss out on the glorious gift of growing in grace, one small step of obedience at a time.

If I were to take inventory of ways I desire to grow in my faithfulness to Jesus, here's what my list would include:

* When I grow up, I'll wake up before the sun rises to feast on God's Word and settle my soul ahead of the day's rush.
* When I grow up, I'll invite my neighbors for a summer barbecue, serving my freshly made tango mint tea, building friendships with them and showing them the unconditional love of Christ.
* When I grow up, I'll be brave enough to start a neighborhood Bible study. We'll spread out our picnic blankets on dewy grass at the park and fix our eyes on the Word while our children play.
* When I grow up, I'll look in the mirror and smile at what I see— a woman made in God's image, created to reflect his glory. Instead of inspecting every flaw, exposed vein, or wrinkle, I'll whisper, "Thank you" to Jesus, who understands the limits of an aging human body.
* When I grow up, instead of proclaiming, "Here, I am!" when walking into a room full of people, I'll see those in front of me and joyfully welcome them with a "There you are" embrace.

No matter how old you are, there's always more spiritual growth to be done. As you continue to grow up, both in age and in your walk with Christ, you'll see that growing in grace is the greatest gift of getting older.

Just because we are still growing up in Christ, that doesn't mean we should put off being faithful to obey the Holy Spirit's prompting now. Why not say yes to his calling today?

Word before World

We keep growing in grace as we seek to be more
like Christ and live in obedience to his calling.

Grow in Grace

Is there an area of delayed obedience in your life?
Is there something God is calling you to that you've been
putting off? Choose faithfulness today, knowing you're
still growing up in Christ as you grow in grace.

42

THE SILENCE OF GOD

For God alone, O my soul, wait in silence,
for my hope is from him.

PSALM 62:5

o our prayers really make a difference in times of crisis? Does God listen when we cry out to him? Does he see our hidden suffering? Does his silence indicate his absence? Or that he is unable to save us?

These questions roll through our minds when disaster pummels our peace, anxiety bulldozes our hope, and the unexpected upends our plans. In times like these, when it seems there's an earthquake in our souls, we have one source of comfort and hope: God's unchanging character as revealed to us in his Word.

The news does not comfort our hearts. The internet does not comfort our hearts. Social media does not comfort our hearts. World leaders do not comfort our hearts. Doctors do not comfort our hearts. Self-help books do not comfort our hearts. Only our God, who is King over everything, can bring true, lasting, indescribable comfort. He teaches us in his Word that he is fully aware of what's happening in the world, and he is at work in ways our human eyes cannot see (see Proverbs 15:3; Hebrews 4:13).

Here's what the Bible reveals about where God is when bad things happen:

✳ **God hears when we call on his name:** "In my distress I called upon the LORD; to my God I cried for help. From his temple he heard my voice, and my cry to him reached his ears" (Psalm 18:6).

✳ **God sees when we suffer and comforts us in affliction:** "Blessed be the God and Father of our Lord Jesus Christ, the Father of mercies and God of all comfort, who comforts us in all our affliction, so that we may be able to comfort those who are in any affliction, with the comfort with which we ourselves are comforted by God" (2 Corinthians 1:3-4).

✳ **God is with us in every trial:** "The nations rage, the kingdoms totter; he utters his voice, the earth melts. The LORD of hosts is with us; the God of Jacob is our fortress" (Psalm 46:6-7).

God's silence does not indicate his absence. Even on the worst days, he listens, responds, and comforts. He provides, delivers, restores, and answers—even if it's not always the way we want or expect. Prayer *does* make a difference, because we serve a loving, powerful God who hears those prayers.

The question is, will we persevere in prayer even when we feel like our words get stuck at the ceiling? Will we come before the Lord earnestly each day? Will we believe his immutable Word, even when our circumstances lead us to doubt? Will we lament with hope, recognizing this broken world is not our forever home and Christ has given us victory through the cross?

There may be over eight billion people inhabiting the earth, but God sees us all. Though we are powerless, he is omnipotent (see Jeremiah 32:17). Though we are unsure what to do, he is all-knowing (see 2 Chronicles 20:12). Though we cannot feel his presence, he is always with us (see Deuteronomy 31:8; Hebrews 13:5). We can wait in silence for him, resting in the assurance that our prayers will reach his heart.

Word before World

God's silence in our suffering doesn't indicate his absence.
Christ suffered on the cross so we can have
hope for eternity and for the present.

Grow in Grace

Is there an area of your life where God seems silent?
Keep praying through your crisis, knowing that God hears,
answers, and offers strength to endure whatever you're facing.

43

CHOOSE JOY TODAY

Rejoice in the Lord always;
again I will say, rejoice.

PHILIPPIANS 4:4

When trials and sorrow come my way,
by God's grace, I'll choose joy today.
Not because life is easy with Jesus,
but because in him I have all I need
to fight this battle victoriously.

With his vision, I can see that he is
working in my time of waiting.
He has always taken what seems bad
and flipped it to be for my good.
So when trials and sorrow head my way,
because of Jesus, I'll choose joy today.

It's not a joy that is oblivious to the harsh realities of life.
It's not a joy that bypasses all hardship or strife.
It's a joy that is rooted deeply in God's lavish grace.
It's a joy that keeps me slowly inching forward in faith.

This unexplainable joy looks to hope yet unseen,
knowing he is with me when I'm in between

a valley and a mountain, a storm and a rainbow,
No—life isn't ever easy, but I trust what he says, so . . .

I'll lean on him when the light is dim,
and I'll trust in him when the future seems bleak.
I'll ask for strength when my soul is weak,
and I'll raise my hands in abundant praise,
as I speak of his joy that is mine today.

Word before World

In Christ, we can count every sorrow and
suffering as joy, knowing that the testing of our
faith produces steadfastness (see James 1:3-5).

Grow in Grace

What circumstances in your life make it difficult
to choose joy? Consider writing a statement or a poem
that proclaims your commitment to follow Jesus and
embrace his joy, even when it doesn't make sense.

44

THE BAROMETER OF YOUR SOUL

Cast your burden on the LORD, and he will sustain you;
he will never permit the righteous to be moved.

PSALM 55:22

Have you ever heard someone predict a storm by the onset of achy joints, back pain, or a throbbing headache? Imagine a seasoned farmer standing on the edge of his freshly plowed field, commenting, "Storm's brewing—I can feel it in my bones." Hours later, rain is falling, thunder is offering a round of applause, and lightning is piercing the darkened sky.

I'm not a farmer or a meteorologist, but almost every time there's a significant change in the weather, I experience a headache that makes my head feel like a lemon being squeezed.

There's a scientific reason some people can feel weather changes within their bodies. The culprit is barometric pressure. When pressure changes cause sudden shifts in weather patterns, many people experience a bodily response. I can't help but think how the same is true for our souls.

When the pressure of life escalates and our inner gauge senses a storm is brewing, we feel it on the inside and the outside. We watch storm clouds barrel toward us in the form of an upcoming surgery, a difficult career decision, an unwanted move, or the end of a relationship. Our bodies shift, along with our hearts and souls, as we brace for the storm. Our shoulder muscles become tangled knots, our chests tighten like an unrelenting lid on a jar of spaghetti sauce, and our heads throb with unmitigated tension. Our flesh and bones signal to our brains that the pressure is rising and we need a safe place to shelter in the storm.

The Gospel of Mark records a windstorm that swept over the Sea of Galilee. Prior to the storm, Jesus and his disciples got on a boat to cross to the other side. While on the boat, Jesus fell asleep on a cushion. Mark writes, "A great windstorm arose, and the waves were breaking into the boat, so that the boat was already filling" (Mark 4:37). The disciples, filled with panic, woke Jesus from his nap. Jesus rebuked the wind saying, "Peace! Be still!"

Immediately, the wind stopped. According to Mark, "There was a great calm" (verse 39).

Can you picture the disciples running around scooping water out of the boat, their bodies tense and their minds flooded with fear, while Jesus slept peacefully? When the pressure rose, the disciples' unbelief was exposed. They believed this storm would be the end of them. Jesus, instead, ended the storm.

If Christ can rest during a storm, so can we. If he could sleep without fear in his fully human body, with his muscles relaxed and his mind at ease, so can we.

When the pressures of life rise, we don't have to cower in fear of the impending storm. Instead, we can rest in our Savior, who is not surprised by the trials we face and who has all power and authority to calm the raging seas. Just as he carried the disciples safely from one side of the lake to the other, so he will carry you.

Word before World

When the pressures of life build,
the safest place to be is in Christ.

Grow in Grace

When sorrow and trials come, cry out to Jesus,
who has the power to calm the raging seas,
including the ones raging in your soul.

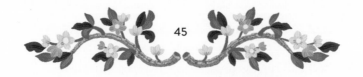

45

THE PRISON CELL OF SICKNESS

I am sure that neither death nor life, nor angels nor rulers,
nor things present nor things to come, nor powers, nor height
nor depth, nor anything else in all creation, will be able to
separate us from the love of God in Christ Jesus our Lord.

ROMANS 8:38-39

There are five hurdles that regularly tempt me to avoid opening God's Word: busyness, laziness, exhaustion, anxiety, and sickness. On any given day, you'll find me attempting to jump over at least one of these hurdles, often tripping on my own shoelaces.

Recently, my family ran smack into the sickness hurdle. With a painful ear infection, a nasty cold, and two children who were battling the same sickness, I found myself drained of joy and endurance. Even though I put my Bible on the bed next to me while I was using a heating pad for my aching ear, I never opened it.

Just before our household succumbed to illness, I read the first chapter of Paul's letter to the church at Philippi. His deepest desire was for God to be glorified in his life and his body no matter what, "whether by life or by death" (Philippians 1:20). The fact that Paul wrote these audacious words while confined to a prison cell is a testimony of God's power at work in him. With chains bruising his wrists, he prayed and declared that even in a prison cell, he would continue to point people to Jesus and praise God for using his suffering to advance the gospel.

If only this were my first response when I come down with an illness or face another trial!

Sickness can feel like a prison, whether it's temporary or long-lasting. The painful surrender of being bedridden inflicts a slow, agonizing blow to our pride and self-sufficiency. But even in sickness, Christ can be glorified.

When we die to our pride, he is glorified.

When we pause to rest, he is glorified.

When we surrender our plans and trust him to give us strength in our weakness, he is glorified.

The trials we endure will not last forever, but the hope of the gospel does. So whether in life or death, in sickness and health, in suffering and rejoicing, in busyness and rest, may Christ be glorified.

The next time you find yourself tripping over hurdles in your path of sanctification, stumble headfirst into the waiting arms of Jesus.

Word before World

Sickness is a classroom where we learn to trust our Savior,
who sympathizes with our suffering
(see Hebrews 4:15).

Grow in Grace

The next time you find yourself sick in bed,
lay aside your pride and surrender to Jesus,
who is still at work while you rest.
Even in those difficult times,
the Lord Jesus will still speak to your heart.

46

HUNGRY FOR GOD

I will be fully satisfied as with the richest of foods;
with singing lips my mouth will praise you.

PSALM 63:5, NIV

"I'm hungry!"

The number of times I hear this phrase from my children each day feels like seventy billion (an exaggeration, but only a slight one!). They are fully cognizant of their rumbling bellies, and they come to me, their mom, for nourishment. If I were to give them a piece of cotton candy each time they approached me, they might be delighted at first, but they'd eventually end up feeling sick and longing for a satisfying meal. However, if I give them a plate of food with protein and the nutrients their bodies need, they will grow and feel healthy.

In our spiritual lives, our hunger can only be satisfied by the filling meat of God's Word. Our spiritual hunger is both satiated *and* heightened by a steady intake of God's Word. As we grow in our faith, so does our love of and our longing for Scripture.

King David experienced ravenous hunger and thirst while in the wilderness. He began Psalm 63 by describing a similar spiritual longing: "O God, you are my God; earnestly I seek you; my soul thirsts for you; my flesh faints for you, as in a dry and weary land where there is no water" (verse 1). David likened his rumbling stomach and his parched mouth to a longing for God. His plea wasn't for a steak dinner or a delicious dessert; it was for the satisfying presence of God. He declared, "My soul will be satisfied as with fat and rich food, and my mouth will praise you with joyful lips" (verse 5).

Hunger is a great soul revealer. When David was hungry and thirsty, his deepest desire was uncovered: he wanted God alone.

Time for a confession: if I skip a meal, I become "hangry"—not the type of person you want to be around. My judgment becomes impaired, and my willingness to stand my ground dissolves under the grumbling of my stomach. The same is often true when I skip spending time with God or taking time to nourish my soul in his presence.

Jesus faced hunger in the wilderness too. He went forty days and forty nights with no food or water (see Matthew 4:1-11). The Maker of the desert was hungry in the desert. The devil tempted Jesus three times, and three times Jesus responded the exact same way: with the tested, true Word of God. The devil couldn't stand against the Scriptures, and he eventually departed from Jesus.

Just as the desert revealed David's longing for God, the desert is where Jesus, God's Son, declared that humans do not live by bread alone but by every word of God. Jesus endured deserts, faced hunger and thirst, and conquered temptation to give us hope in our own wastelands.

Because of Christ, we can join David and pray, "Because your steadfast love is better than life, my lips will praise you" (Psalm 63:3).

Word before World

What we hunger for is revealed in hardship.
When we hunger for God, our souls will be truly satisfied.

Grow in Grace

What does your soul crave in times of emotional or spiritual hunger?
What would it look like to feed your craving for more of Jesus?
Read Psalm 63 and write verse 3 in a place you'll see it often.

47

THE PERFECT DAY

I saw a new heaven and a new earth, for the first heaven and
the first earth had passed away, and the sea was no more.

REVELATION 21:1

On a recent Wednesday morning, I saw a forecast that the weather would be a perfect ten out of ten on their rating scale. Naturally, I had to check it out for myself. I loaded my daughter into our pink jogging stroller to go for a walk and enjoy this so-called perfect day.

As I walked down the street beneath a row of maple trees, I soaked in every detail. Tree limbs were budding with infant leaves, their lime green color so bright it almost looked fluorescent. Birds whistled cheerfully, fluttering from branch to branch as if playing a game of hide-and-seek. A gentle breeze tickled my skin, sunlight danced through the trees, and the sky was a shocking shade of blue. It really did feel like the *perfect* day.

Have you ever experienced one of those days when the weather is so delightful you open every window to bring the glorious outdoors inside? Maybe you opt for a picnic dinner to stay outside longer, or maybe you let the kids stay up to enjoy the beautiful evening.

As perfect as days like this seem, though, we know all is not truly perfect in this world. Even when our surroundings are ideal, someone somewhere is trying to break out of crippling depression. Someone is trembling while holding the phone, listening to the doctor's devastating diagnosis.

Someone is barely holding on to hope as they break apart lies that have haunted them since childhood. For some, the so-called ten out of ten day is in no way perfect, and the beautiful weather seems more like a taunt than a promise.

In Randy Alcorn's book *Heaven*, he writes, "The world as it was, and the world as it will be, is exceedingly good. The world *as it is now*, inhabited by humanity *as we are now*, is twisted. But this is a temporary condition, with an eternal remedy: Christ's redemptive work."[1] The perfect day on earth does not even come close to the glory we will experience in the new heaven and the new earth, where we will dwell in the presence of God for all eternity.

One day soon, all who have placed their faith in Jesus will enjoy eternity in his perfect presence. What we see on earth's best days is only a glimpse of the glory to come. And what we experience on the worst days is a reminder of what we have been saved from.

So when you experience a rare ten out of ten day, look forward to spending eternity with God on the new earth—exploring and fellowshiping, enjoying and worshiping him. At the same time, look in front of you and remember that although we are not there yet, God has abundantly provided beauty all around us—a reflection of Jesus, who is the only true source of perfection.

Word before World
The best days we experience on earth do not
compare to the glory of heaven.

Grow in Grace
The next time you experience an ideal day,
imagine the new heaven and the new earth and
praise God for glimpses of glory that point us to eternity.

48

ONE STEP AT A TIME

We walk by faith, not by sight.

2 CORINTHIANS 5:7

Faith is not following a detailed road map to a final destination. Faith is trusting God to guide and provide, one step at a time.

Throughout Scripture, God's perfectly timed guidance weaves through each narrative as he faithfully leads his people. The Old Testament is chock-full of examples of God's guidance, despite his people's faithlessness and rebellion.

During the time when the judges ruled, the Israelites asked God to give them a king so they could be like other nations (see 1 Samuel 8:4-22). They were unhappy with God as their ruler and rebelled against his leadership. God gave them what they wanted by appointing Saul as their king. Saul was a warrior who was handsome in appearance but a coward at heart.

Early in King Saul's reign, he disobeyed God's commands, including his instruction to completely destroy the Amalekites. In response, God rejected Saul as king. Samuel, the prophet who had anointed Saul, grieved over Saul, and then he completed the task Saul failed to do (see 1 Samuel 15:32-33).

Samuel's heart was still mourning for Saul when the Lord instructed him, "How long will you grieve over Saul, since I have rejected him from being king over Israel? Fill your horn with oil, and go. I will send you to Jesse the Bethlehemite, for I have provided for myself a king among his sons" (1 Samuel 16:1). Fear struck Samuel when he heard God's command. He knew that if he anointed a new king and Saul heard about it, he would be killed (verse 2).

God didn't answer Samuel with step-by-step instructions outlining the final outcome; he simply told Samuel the next right thing to do. He assured him, "I will show you what you shall do" (verse 3). Laying aside his fear of Saul and potential death, Samuel followed God, one step at a time. God guided him through a series of divine circumstances to a ruddy young shepherd who would become the next king of Israel—none other than King David (verse 13).

Samuel's humble faith in God's provision led him to God's chosen candidate, the very king whose offspring would include the promised Messiah, Jesus (see 2 Samuel 7:12-16; Matthew 1:1). His honest, faith-fueled obedience reminds us that God's plans are perfect—beyond what our human minds can comprehend (see Isaiah 55:8-9). Though we do not have step-by-step directions to follow, we serve the same God who led Samuel to David. So often we pray for detailed instructions about what we should do next, only to be discouraged when that's not what we receive. But God hasn't left us on our own. We have his Word—his perfect track record that details his providence throughout history.

The careful guidance God showed to Samuel in anointing David is just one of countless examples in Scripture spotlighting God's faithfulness. We have the benefit of hindsight as we read God's Word. As we walk by faith, not by sight, we can keep in mind God's consistent character and mysterious ways (see 2 Corinthians 5:7). The faith Samuel displayed as he followed God's leading is the same faith we cling to as we obey his Word and follow him.

We may not have a detailed road map to follow as we navigate life's tough decisions. But we know our final destination, and we have his Word to strengthen us each step of the way.

So walk by faith, not by sight, as you live for his Kingdom, and trust him to guide and provide—one step at a time.

Word before World
Faith is trusting God to provide every step of the journey.

Grow in Grace
In what area of your life are you in need of God's direction?
What would it look like for you to surrender the end
result to him and take the first step of obedience?

49

WHEN YOUR HEART CONDEMNS YOU

There is therefore now no condemnation
for those who are in Christ Jesus.

ROMANS 8:1

Do you keep a record of your wrongs? Maybe you won't let go of the times you lost your temper with your children or your husband, envied your friend's success, or complained about your circumstances. It comes more naturally for us to carry around the weight of our failures than it does to come to Christ in repentance and receive his forgiveness. We often walk around shackled to shame, carrying the gargantuan boulder of condemnation.

When we define who we are by our failures, we run on a hamster wheel of unending accusations. But God tells us over and over in his Word that he will extend grace to his children who come to him in repentance.

In the book of Lamentations, Jeremiah grieved over Israel's unrepentant sin, which led to the fall of Judah. God warned his people: if they did not repent, turn from their sin, and obey him, they would be judged and receive just punishment. In his faithfulness, God fulfilled this promise.

Rarely do we pair God's faithfulness with his judgment, but Lamentations 2:17 explains, "The LORD has done what he planned; he has fulfilled his word" (NIV). God is perfectly holy and just, and at the same time, he is forgiving and merciful to those who repent and return to him. He is faithful to judge sin according to his holiness, but he is also faithful to extend mercy to the repentant.

We can join Jeremiah in proclaiming, "Because of the LORD's great love we are not consumed, for his compassions never fail. They are new every morning; great is your faithfulness" (Lamentations 3:22-23, NIV). The kingdom of Judah should have been condemned because of the people's sin, but because of God's great love and unfailing compassion, they received his mercy and were not consumed.

When we have a repentant heart, we can rejoice in God's fresh mercy every morning and be released from the prison of condemnation.

So when your mind begins to recite the record of your wrongs and becomes ensnared by condemnation and accusations, come before God in repentance and receive the rest extended to you through Christ (see Matthew 4:17; 11:28-30).

Jesus suffered for our sins on the cross. He took on the judgment we rightly deserve and rose again, conquering sin and death, so we can confidently believe with full assurance, "There is therefore now *no condemnation* for those who are in Christ Jesus" (Romans 8:1, emphasis added).

If you feel consumed by your failures today and your record of wrongs is a mile long, turn your eyes upon Jesus, who fulfilled God's promises and forgives our sins. His mercies are new every morning, and by his grace, we are not consumed—or condemned.

Word before World
Condemnation has been crushed by Christ's death on the cross.
Our God is faithful to give us new mercies every day.

Grow in Grace
Confess your list of wrongs to the Lord, and picture Jesus
nailing each one to the cross. Ask for his forgiveness,
and embrace the new mercies offered to you in Christ.

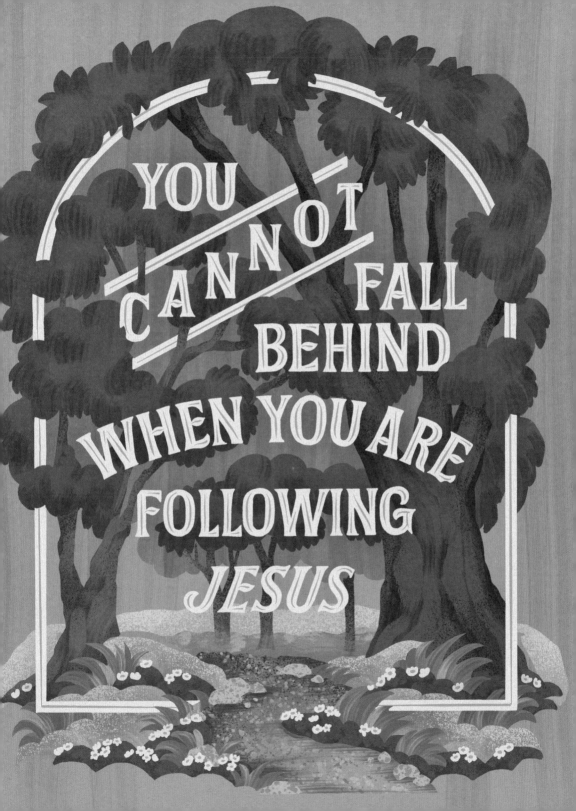

50

FUELED BY GRACE

The LORD is my portion;
I promise to keep your words.
PSALM 119:57

This may surprise you, but there is a subtle danger in making it a goal to read the Bible every day. In our humanity, we can easily make consistent Bible study a way to earn God's love. Instead of reading the Bible out of love and delight, we see this time as something to check off a spiritual to-do list. As a goal setter myself, I'm prone to finding my worth in what I achieve—and this bleeds into my walk with God.

For those of us who love making goals, the thrill of placing a checkmark next to an item on a list never gets old. The first time I read through the Bible in a year, I took great pride in what I'd accomplished. I began the marathon and miraculously finished it.

Goal complete—*check*.

The next year I decided to start again, but life's challenges reared up and I quickly fell behind. My perfectionism shouted through a megaphone, "You're failing at following God!" The glaring unchecked boxes on my Bible-reading plan discouraged me from continuing, and I gave up.

We must be aware of three dangerous heart postures when we approach Bible reading:

1. **Our Scripture reading is motivated by pride**. It becomes more about our own spiritual performance and accomplishments than about loving God.

2. **Our Scripture reading is motivated by fear.** We worry that God will love us less if we don't meet a certain standard and stay up-to-date with our reading plan. We might read with the wrong intent— to be better and to accomplish more, rather than to know God more. The goal becomes completion, not knowing, communing with, and delighting in God.

3. **Our Scripture reading is motivated by perfectionism.** If we fall behind, our gut response is to throw in the towel instead of running to the throne of grace for help and mercy (see Hebrews 4:16).

The goal of reading God's Word is not to puff up our souls or to place a big checkmark at the end of the year. It's not to add to our "Christian résumé" or earn God's favor. The aim is to know Christ and exalt him in our lives as we come before him hungry for truth and humbled by his grace. The goal is to glorify him through our fervent reading, joy-filled worship, and faithful obedience. And this is something that cannot be measured.

If you find yourself reading God's Word with the wrong motivations or you're tempted to quit when you miss a day or two (or even a month!), don't let that stop you from pursuing the discipline of daily Bible reading! God gives more grace to those who draw near to him (see James 4:6-7). His words don't have a return address; they always accomplish what he sets out for them to do (see Isaiah 55:10-11).

So make it your aim to read the Word each day in order to know God and delight in him. And on the days when your Bible remains unopened, don't quit or listen to the voice of perfectionism shouting in your ear. Surrender your checklists to God, and seek to know him each time you open the Word. Anytime is the right time to read the Word.

Word before World

The goal of reading God's Word is not
to check an item off your to-do list;
it is to know God more.

Grow in Grace

Pray Psalm 119:18 as you read God's Word:
"Open my eyes that I may behold
wondrous things out of your law."

YOU ARE WEAK, BUT HE IS STRONG

For the sake of Christ, then, I am content with weaknesses,
insults, hardships, persecutions, and calamities.
For when I am weak, then I am strong.

2 CORINTHIANS 12:10

Weak is not a word I'd like to use to describe myself, but the reality is, most days I feel more weak than I do strong. I'm well aware of the myriad ways I fall short, mess up, and fail to follow through. In my human nature, I'm needy, limited, and frail. But I am learning, like the apostle Paul, to boast in my weaknesses.

Paul had an impressive religious résumé, one that set him apart from other educated Roman citizens (see 2 Corinthians 11). Even so, he was keenly aware of his weaknesses, frailty, and shortcomings. This awareness of his limitations did not stop him from preaching the gospel or ministering in the name of Jesus; instead, it tethered him more closely to Christ.

On paper, Paul appeared to have his life together—a high achiever, someone who was well connected, a man of vast knowledge. And yet he confessed that he had been pierced by a thorn in the flesh, "a messenger of Satan to harass me, to keep me from becoming conceited" (2 Corinthians 12:7). Paul begged the Lord three times to remove this thorn, which no doubt wounded his pride and hindered his sense of self-sufficiency. But the Lord revealed to him, "My grace is sufficient for you, for my power is made perfect in weakness" (verse 9).

Instead of arguing about other thornless ways God could reveal his power,

Paul accepted his limitation and boasted about his weaknesses so the strength of Christ would be revealed through him (verse 9). This is the paradox of what it means to be strong as a Christian: when we are weak, *he* is strong.

Running from our weaknesses is not the remedy to become strong in Christ. Trying harder and pushing further is not the key to unlocking Christ's power in us. The power of Christ belongs to those who accept their weakness as a means to grace—to those who rely not on themselves but on him alone (see Psalm 62:5-8).

Boasting in our weaknesses goes against human nature, but with the Holy Spirit's help, we can accept our thorns and limitations as a means to experience the power of Christ. We boast about our weaknesses when we humbly admit that we don't keep the world spinning; God does.

When we embrace the thorn that pierces our hearts and presses into our flesh as a gift of grace, we receive God's power and live with supernatural strength—even in our frailty. From this posture of humility, with thorns wounding our pride and limiting our self-sufficiency, we learn the joyful surrender of relying on Christ alone.

Come to Christ as a weak vessel—wounded yet whole, pierced yet strong—knowing that your Savior wore a crown of thorns in your place. When you are weak, he is strong.

Word before World

Running from our weaknesses will never make us strong.
The power of Christ belongs to those who accept their
weaknesses as a means of grace and rely on Christ alone.

Grow in Grace

In your journal, write down a list of your weaknesses. Next to
each one, write how you've seen God's faithfulness in giving you
strength to overcome and to continue fighting the good fight.

WHEN SILENCE IS UNSETTLING

Be still, and know that I am God. I will be exalted
among the nations, I will be exalted in the earth!

PSALM 46:10

ave you ever opened your Bible during a rare moment of quiet, only to feel like an inner hurricane has let loose? Instead of enjoying the moment of respite, you find yourself craving being busy over being still.

Sometimes, the silence we experience when reading the Word of God is unsettling. Especially during busy seasons, our souls can become so accustomed to noise that we struggle to be still before the Lord.

There are times when I sit down to pray or read God's Word, and the sound of deafening silence thrashes inside my soul. I crave moments of quiet, but when one comes, I find I'm more comfortable with white noise from the hustle and bustle of my daily routine. The hush of silence amplifies the chaos in my head.

When I can finally be still, all I want to do is get moving again. I'm anxious to silence the thoughts that remind me of everything out of my control. I'm willing to do anything to avoid the questions plaguing my soul or the convictions nagging my conscience.

Maybe you've felt this same sense of discomfort. Adrenaline pumps through your veins to help you accomplish what needs to be done, making it hard to linger in God's Word or still your thoughts to meditate on his truths. Once you finally have a moment to think, your mind is bombarded with questions like *What if . . . ?*, *What now?*, *Why not?*, or *Why this?* No matter how hard you try, you can't focus or sit still. You're craving peace, but instead, you feel stuck, unsettled, and undone.

Silence surrounds you, but chaos stirs inside of you.

This is nothing new to God. His people have always navigated the tension between longing for stillness and balking at it. The prophet Isaiah told the Israelites, "Thus said the Lord GOD, the Holy One of Israel, 'In returning and rest you shall be saved; in quietness and in trust shall be your strength.' But you were unwilling, and you said, 'No! We will flee upon horses; therefore you shall flee away'" (Isaiah 30:15-16).

God urged his people to be quiet, to silence their noise, and to trust in him. But they were unwilling.

And, often, we are unwilling too.

The holy one, the creator of our bones, brains, and bodies, knows what we need. He invites us to return to him, enjoy the rest he gives, and receive his supernatural strength (see Psalm 116:7). His Word calms our souls, transforms our worries into worship, and infuses hope into our hearts. But first, we must be willing to slow down and receive it.

We are like the Israelites—searching for comfort, peace, and rest from something we can physically hold on to. But God, like a father caring for his beloved child, invites us to sit in silence, stillness, and surrender.

Silence strips us of our self-sufficiency and reveals our desperate need for God. Being still before him hurts at times, but it also heals the soul wounds we try to bandage and drown out with noise. Unsettling silence can be a gift from God, a reminder that nothing and no one else can satisfy the ache in our souls.

In the uncomfortable quiet, bring your heart, body, mind, and soul before him, and be willing to receive his rest.

Word before World
Stillness reveals our need for God's
presence, peace, and strength.

Grow in Grace
When was the last time you were silent before God?
Set aside a few minutes today to be still before
him in prayer, solitude, and worship.

53

FIGHT FROM VICTORY

Take the helmet of salvation, and the sword of the Spirit,
which is the word of God.

EPHESIANS 6:17

Starting the day without Jesus is like going to battle without a sword—it doesn't end well. I should know; I've done it countless times.

Instead of putting the Word before the world, I grab my phone first to scroll social media or answer emails, or I press snooze several times and start the day rushed and unprepared. Sometimes, by midday, I wonder why I feel so off, only to realize I didn't settle my soul in the Lord. I went to battle without a sword.

The lure of a quick check-in online or a few minutes on social media is tantalizing. Like moths to a flame, we are drawn to what's shiny rather than what's best for our souls. Without even being conscious of it, we start and end our days by *checking out* of life rather than *checking in* with God. But praise God, one moment in the Word has the power to change our entire outlook.

God's Word is more than a book to collect dust on your nightstand; it's a weapon God has equipped us with to fight the enemy's lies and replace them with gospel truth. Paul encouraged believers to put on the whole armor of God and live in the victory of Jesus (see John 16:33; Ephesians 6:10-17). Each day when we get dressed, the most important thing we can put on is God's otherworldly, impenetrable armor.

The battle we fight is not against other people or illness or potential catastrophe, but "against the rulers, against the authorities, against the cosmic powers over this present darkness" (Ephesians 6:12). We do not fight in our own strength but in the perfect strength of Christ. Putting on God's armor enables us to stand up and "fight the good fight of the faith" rather than retreat in fear (1 Timothy 6:12).

In the list of the armor God has provided for his people—the belt of truth, the breastplate of righteousness, the feet fitted with the readiness of the gospel of peace, the helmet of salvation, and the shield of faith—the only tool of offense is the sword of the Spirit. We protect ourselves from Satan's flaming arrows with the armor, and we counterattack with the sword of the Spirit, the living and active Word of God (see Hebrews 4:12).

No matter how your morning started today, center *this moment* around Jesus. Open your Bible and pray God's life-giving, soul-piercing Word. Slip your arm into the shield of faith. Put on the breastplate of righteousness, and stand firm in what you know to be true in God's Word. Move forward in faith, with the gospel of peace springing in your steps. And most important, don't forget to bring your sword to defeat every lie and discouragement the enemy sends your way.

As a child of God, you fight *from* victory, not *for* victory, and he has already given you everything you need for this day and this life, right on the pages of his Word.

Word before World

God's Word is the offensive weapon we use
to fight Satan's attacks. His flaming arrows are
his impenetrable promises, piercing every lie.

Grow in Grace

What battle are you fighting today? Don't go to battle
without your sword. Meditate on God's Word,
and fight from the victory you have in Christ!

54

EVERY HOUR I NEED THEE

As for me, I am poor and needy, but the Lord takes thought for me.
You are my help and my deliverer; do not delay, O my God!

PSALM 40:17

The moment I wake up, my mind floods with thoughts. My chest tightens with concerns about the day ahead, plans for what needs to be done, and lingering to-dos left from yesterday's list. I'm a recovering perfectionist, still learning how to loosen my white-knuckled grip on the plans I make and hand them to the Lord. My worries try to convince me I am self-sufficient and capable of holding the world together, but they actually reveal that I am incredibly needy.

Hymn writer Annie Sherwood Hawks was a wife and mother to three young children in the late 1800s. With a busy family and home life, Annie was regularly reminded of her need for God's help. Instead of relying on systems, life hacks, and perfectly planned schedules, she relied on the presence of the Lord to fuel her days and guide her steps.

One day, as she was going about her tasks, she became utterly "filled with the sense of nearness to the Master" and wondered "how one could live without Him."[1] She penned these lines in response:

I need thee every hour,
*   most gracious Lord;*
no tender voice like thine
*   can peace afford.*

I need thee, O I need thee;
every hour I need thee;
O bless me now, my Savior,
I come to thee.

In the middle of her ordinary day, God lifted the veil from her eyes, and she was overcome with her great need for him. This pivotal moment sparked a worship service in her heart that reverberates throughout churches centuries later.

When my mind is bombarded with the needs and demands around me or when my heart looks at the tasks before me with disdain, her lyrics echo in my ears. God beckons me to pray, plead, and sing, "I need thee, O I need thee; *every hour* I need thee."

It is a sheer gift when God opens our eyes to our neediness. When we live as if we hold the world together, we miss the joy of knowing the one who actually does. The truth is, we need God every hour, every minute, every millisecond.

We need him to open our eyes to behold his grace when all is going well, and we need him to hold us together when everything is falling apart. We need him to keep us levelheaded when our dreams are fulfilled, and we need him to sustain us when our worst nightmare comes true.

Blessed is the woman who recognizes her desperate need for God. She will scrub dishes, run errands, complete her projects, and do the one-millionth load of laundry with a keen awareness that God is with her, and her heart will be filled with joy.

Word before World
It is a good thing to be needy for God.

Grow in Grace
The next time you feel overwhelmed, sing this simple
prayer of surrender: "I need thee every hour."

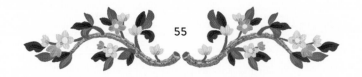

55

EVERY TEAR MATTERS

He will wipe away every tear from their eyes, and death
shall be no more, neither shall there be mourning, nor crying,
nor pain anymore, for the former things have passed away.

REVELATION 21:4

I once believed tears were a sign of weakness. I vividly remember a moment when I felt the aching pang of heartbreak, and someone jokingly asked, "Are you going to cry now?"

I consciously kept my pent-up tears from flowing, embarrassed to show my weakness. Like pressing a cork into a shaken-up bottle to keep it from exploding, I stuffed down my unshed tears in an effort to look strong.

Years later, the pressure built and the cork finally blew off. After adding our first son to our family, I didn't ease my prior commitments and continued to work, travel, and lead my Bible study group as if I had no limitations. One year into motherhood, my body and mind broke down, and the tears finally began to flow. God used that season to bring me to this realization: I am not made to bottle my tears but to let their healing flow point me to God, my true healer.

Suppressing my tears had kept me from coming to God in my brokenness and profound need. I thought my stoicism was a sign of strength, but in reality, my refusal to cry out in my grief and pain had hindered my healing and freedom.

As the tears finally came out over the following days and weeks, I learned that God is not put off by our cries for help. Psalm 56:8 tells us he holds our tears in a bottle—he sees every drop that falls.

God made our bodies to produce tears for a reason. Tears are not a sign of weakness; they can be an act of worshipful surrender. When we pray and tears stream down our faces, we can open our clenched fists, release our worries, and be reminded of God's nearness. When we weep and lament over injustice, our tears reveal how God moves our hearts to action. When we speak about what he has done and our eyes sting with tears of gratitude, or when we sing about God's faithfulness while crying tears of joy, we are prompted to a deeper awe of and love for God. When we repent over our sins and cry out our confession, our tears expose our change of heart.

Every tear counts. Every tear matters.

There will be a day when every tear will be wiped away, but today is not that day (see Ecclesiastes 3:4; Revelation 21:4). In the meantime, God is faithful to rescue and redeem our broken parts and hold our tearstained faces.

Don't ignore your tears, and don't hold them back. Let them flow freely, whether they're tears of sorrow and grief or joy and thanksgiving. Cry out to God, and find hope as your tears fall in the presence of the one who knows your sorrow firsthand: Jesus, "a man of sorrows and acquainted with grief" (Isaiah 53:3).

Word before World

God sees our tears of grief, pain, joy, and praise,
and he tenderly preserves them in his bottle.

Grow in Grace

Pay attention to your tears. The next time you feel like
crying, let your tears flow in surrender and praise to God,
who holds each one and offers you hope in Jesus.

SWEETER THAN HONEY

Oh, taste and see that the LORD is good!
Blessed is the man who takes refuge in him!
PSALM 34:8

As a writer, it pains me to admit this, but I didn't enjoy reading when I was younger. Most books I ingested were read aloud to me by my ever-so-patient mother, who helped me finish my reading assignments for school. It wasn't until my early twenties that I developed a ravenous hunger for reading. This hunger was stirred in me by a mentor whose love for God's Word was contagious.

Seated on the carpet in her lime-green living room, I took in God's Word as if my mentor were spooning the most delectable honey into my mouth. Alongside other women, ranging from twenty-somethings to women with graying hair, I tasted the sweetness of God's Word. I've been hungry for it ever since.

In the children's book *The Bee Tree*, a little girl named Mary Ellen doesn't like to read, so her grandfather takes her on a bee hunt. They find several honeybees and begin to follow their zigzag, loop-de-loop path to the hive. Along the way, onlookers, friends, and neighbors join the adventure, following the bees to their home.

In the end, the group arrives at the bee tree and gathers honey from the hive. Back home, the little girl's grandfather takes a spoonful of the honey they collected from their journey and drips it onto a book for her to taste and savor.

"There is such sweetness inside of that book too! . . . Such things . . .

adventure, knowledge, and wisdom. . . . Just like we ran after the bees to find their tree, so you must also chase these things through the pages of a book!" he urges the little girl. And that is exactly what she does.[1]

When I read this book for the first time to my boys, I couldn't help but think about the Book containing words that are sweeter than honey. The psalmist writes, "How sweet are your words to my taste, sweeter than honey to my mouth!" (Psalm 119:103). The more we taste the precious words of God, the more the rest of the world loses its flavor. God's Word changes our spiritual tastebuds and satisfies our hungry souls.

Like the little girl in *The Bee Tree*, we must learn to chase after God's Word more than anything else. To know God's Word is to know him. To delight in God's Word is to delight in him. To taste the sweetness of God's Word is to enjoy his goodness. But we cannot know him, delight in him, or taste his goodness if we do not open our mouths for him to drip the honey of his Word into. Of all the words in the world, among the millions of books written, none compare to the Word of God. Surround yourself with his Word and with others who desire God's Word. Together, you can journey toward the cross, the tree Jesus hung on so you could taste the sweetness of salvation.

Chase after the treasures in Scripture, where you will find the greatest adventure as you follow Christ. Savor your Savior as you taste and see that he is the definition of all that is good and sweet.

Word before World
God's Word is sweeter than the sweetest honey.

Grow in Grace
If you are able to, grab a spoonful of honey to savor as you read Psalm 34. Allow the sweetness of the bees' nectar to instill in you a tangible reminder of the sweetness of God's Word.

57

A RIVER RUNS THROUGH YOU

Jesus said to her, "Everyone who drinks of this water will be thirsty again,
but whoever drinks of the water that I will give him will never
be thirsty again. The water that I will give him will become
in him a spring of water welling up to eternal life."

JOHN 4:13-14

In the beginning, God planted a garden. And like a good gardener, he provided the perfect environment for his garden to flourish. Genesis describes a river that "flowed out of Eden to water the garden" (Genesis 2:10).

After the Fall, God banished Adam and Eve from the Garden of Eden, appointing cherubim and a flaming sword to guard the tree of life (see Genesis 3:23-24). Ever since, humankind has been searching for Eden, longing for a drink from the river of God to quench our thirst, searching in all the wrong places for satisfaction.

We take our empty cups to different streams, yearning for a sip to satisfy our discontented souls. We dip them into the trickle of worldly affirmation, only to discover that the drops of water dry up before they even reach our tongues. We beg for a drink from the well of achievement, only to find that it's shallow and unable to quench our thirst. We search for streams in status, appearance, relationships, or financial security, hoping to find something that will satisfy us, but we come up empty-handed.

Just as a garden cannot flourish without God's provision, we cannot flourish when we are not in him.

As we hold empty cups in our hands, God calls to us, "Come, everyone who thirsts, come to the waters; and he who has no money, come, buy and eat! Come, buy wine and milk without money and without price" (Isaiah 55:1). The invitation couldn't be more enticing: come and drink from God's river of grace *for free*! Soak up his salvation through Christ Jesus and find true satisfaction forever!

Christ is the river of living water that always satisfies and never runs dry. Not only does he fill our empty cups, but he makes them overflow (see Psalm 23:5; John 4:14; 7:37-39). When we drink deeply from the well of God, he makes his river of grace run through us, a steady stream of living water that flows from Christ alone. We still experience spiritual dryness as we endure life in the desert outside the Garden of Eden, but a new eternal garden awaits, where the "river of the water of life, bright as crystal" flows directly from the throne of God (Revelation 22:1-2).

So bring your empty cup to Christ, the living water, who satisfies our souls and leads us on paths of righteousness (see Psalm 23). When the heat of life makes you thirsty, drink deeply from the well of God's Word. In Christ, a river runs through you, leading straight back to him.

Word before World
Christ is the living water that always
satisfies and never runs dry.

Grow in Grace
Think through your day and note the times that
feel most draining for your soul. What would it look
like to integrate the deep refreshment of reading
God's Word into that part of your day?

139

58

TRUE REST

In peace I will both lie down and sleep;
for you alone, O LORD, make me dwell in safety.

PSALM 4:8

I collapsed onto my bed, mentally and physically exhausted, grabbed my phone from the bedside table, and started scrolling. It was the first time that day I'd been able to come to a complete stop, and my soul—weary from the day's demands—craved a distraction. I might not have consciously recognized it, but I was attempting to escape my weariness, weakness, and worn-out reality.

As I pulled up social media, this thought came into my mind, stopping me in my tracks: *True rest is not found in scrolling social media; it's found in surrendering to the embrace of my Savior.*

What I needed at that moment could not be found in posts, pictures, articles, or captions. It wouldn't be found in shopping for new clothes or getting tips about having a clean and tidy home. Refreshing rest—the kind my body, soul, and mind desperately need—comes from Christ alone.

I wish I could say that every time I'm given the opportunity to rest, I choose to do what stirs my affection for Christ, but most often, I choose what's convenient. Instead of reaching for my Bible, talking to God in prayer, or even closing my eyes and releasing every tense muscle in his presence, I run to whatever might seem like a quick fix for the stress wreaking havoc in my body.

Throughout his life, David cried out to God in his distress. David was well acquainted with stress. He had been slandered, betrayed, and relentlessly pursued by oppressors. In his exhaustion, he turned toward God, who gives relief from the pressures that squeeze us like sponges. Rather than running to a quick fix for relief, David ran to God in prayer.

By the end of his song, David conceded, "In peace I will both lie down and sleep; for you alone, O LORD, make me dwell in safety." David knew that true rest is found in surrendering to God, who gives us true relief.

The next time you collapse onto your bed with a heavy heart and a burdened soul, redirect your gaze to Jesus and surrender to his loving arms. Remember, the same God who comforted and kept David is the same God who provides us with rest at the start and end of a long, hard day—and during all the moments in between.

Word before World

Rest is a gift from God—one we receive
by surrendering our fears, worries, and problems
and relaxing in the loving embrace of Christ.

Grow in Grace

What do you turn to for an escape from exhaustion?
In moments of reset, instead of turning to your phone, TV,
or anything else that dulls your affection for Christ, breathe
deeply and relax your muscles and your mind in him.

59

THE COURAGE TO PRAY

This is my prayer: that your love may abound more and
more in knowledge and depth of insight, so that you may be
able to discern what is best and may be pure and blameless for
the day of Christ, filled with the fruit of righteousness that
comes through Jesus Christ—to the glory and praise of God.

PHILIPPIANS 1:9-11

I'm chopping carrots for soup, my head tilted as I balance the phone on my shoulder—multitasking, as usual. It's been ages since I've talked to my friend, and at this point, we are living completely different lives from when we first met. Hers is brimming with excitement and new adventures; mine is filled with never-ending laundry and carrots to chop.

As we chat, I drop the carrots into the stew and catch myself growing envious of her success. I compare what God has called me to in this season to what God has called her to, and my life seems more, well, ordinary.

Later that evening, as I'm scrubbing the soup pot, God scrubs my soul.

I know he has not called me to compare my life to my friend; he has called me to pray for her. He has not called me to compete with other women; he has called me to be faithful to complete the tasks he has placed before me and to love those around me. Sulking over my ordinary circumstances won't free me from the comparison boiling inside me.

Rather, freedom is found in courageously praying for the advancement of God's Kingdom—and even for the blessing of my sister in Christ.

In Paul's letter to the church at Philippi, he writes, "I thank my God in all my remembrance of you, always in every prayer of mine for you all making my prayer with joy, because of your partnership in the gospel from the first day until now." He goes on to say, "It is my prayer that your love may abound more and more, with knowledge and all discernment, so that you may approve what is excellent, and so be pure and blameless for the day of Christ, filled with the fruit of righteousness that comes through Jesus Christ, to the glory and praise of God" (Philippians 1:3-5, 9-11).

Paul's courageous, humble prayer for the believers at Philippi was for their blessing, the growth of their love for Christ, and their advancement in ministry. He held them in his heart as beloved brothers and sisters, not as sources of competition or comparison. This is especially admirable considering Paul wrote his letter while chained in a prison cell. He was being held captive; they were free, yet he was driven not by jealousy but by fervent love for Christ and his church.

What would happen if we dared to follow in Paul's Christ-centered footsteps, celebrating when the gospel is proclaimed, whether it's through our own lips and lives or through the lips and lives of others?

If our heart's desire is to know Christ and make him known, we must humbly realize this will happen through us *and* our brothers and sisters in Christ. When we pray for the blessing of others' ministries and for the growth of their love and knowledge of Christ, we play a role in advancing the gospel—which is our ultimate aim as believers.

Are you brave enough to pray for the blessing of others, trusting that God won't pass you by?

Are you humble enough to cherish the gifts of others, cheering them on in the race they run as you run the race set before you?

Pray for the blessing of others, dear friend. God won't pass you by.

Word before World

The same God who is at work in your life is working
in the lives of your brothers and sisters in Christ.

Grow in Grace

Pray for a friend today and send her a message,
letting her know you're praying for her.

IN CHRIST YOU ARE FULLY LOVED FULLY FREE FULLY HIS

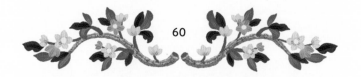

60

WITH US IN THE WILDERNESS

The LORD your God has blessed you in all the work of your hands.
He knows your going through this great wilderness. These forty years
the LORD your God has been with you. You have lacked nothing.

DEUTERONOMY 2:7

f you were to make a timeline of your life, what would you include? What major events, moves, accomplishments, and life stages would serve as markers on your journey? What trials, losses, heartaches, and crushed dreams would indicate forks in the road? Each of us has a story, layered with unique complications, challenges, and celebrations.

The story of the Israelites' long, tumultuous journey from Egypt to the land of milk and honey is as layered as a slice of baklava! Moses recorded each step of their expedition, noting their starting place, their campsites, and the major events that unfolded along the way. Numbers 33 is written with a repetitive framework: "And they set out from [location] and camped at [location]." Over and over, Moses painstakingly detailed the names and places the Israelites journeyed through as the next generation prepared to conquer Canaan.

Moses knew how quickly God's people tended to forget his faithfulness in the past. He knew that in order for them to move forward in faith and conquer the Promised Land, they would need to look back and see all the ways God had been with them in the wilderness.

Moses describes their journey this way: "You have lacked nothing"

(Deuteronomy 2:7). In all their years as nomads, without a place to call home, they had everything they needed. Their shoes did not wear out, and their bellies did not go unfilled. Though God's provision looked different from their shortsighted desires at times, he provided exactly what they needed.

Life often feels like endless wandering in the wilderness. We set out for one place and end up in another. We desire one thing, and God gives us something else. We want the land of milk and honey without the long journey to get there.

Moses reminded the Israelites, and he reminds us today, that God is with us in the wilderness and to be with God is to be home. Knowing that God sees the path we take, the heartaches we experience, the disappointments we carry, and the adversity we endure, we can set out on the journey before us with confidence.

As you look back on your layered life through eyes of faith, you will see how, even in your wandering, you lacked nothing (see Psalm 23:1). And you will taste how sweet God's presence and provision have been—even better than the best piece of baklava.

Word before World

Our journey in life is rarely linear, but God lovingly
guides us along the twists and turns.

Grow in Grace

Make a simple timeline of your life. Looking back on
the formative events, how can you see God's hand at
work in various moves, transitions, and changes?

61

GOD'S TRACK RECORD

If we are faithless, he remains faithful—
for he cannot deny himself.

2 TIMOTHY 2:13

I live in a land of hypotheticals, always thinking up the worst-case scenario of what could happen, sometimes envisioning what could be, play by play, in an attempt to brace myself for potential impact. I pray for God to hear, guide, answer, and provide while also wondering what I'll do if he doesn't.

When we dwell in the land of hypotheticals, we hyperfocus on the future and suffer from spiritual amnesia—forgetting God's past faithfulness and bypassing his promises.

And when we suffer from spiritual amnesia, it's hard to trust God with what tomorrow holds. Our minds become so fixated on making plans that we forget God's grace and his promises to sustain us—no matter what comes.

If you are having trouble recalling God's promises, start here:

1. **Review God's track record in Scripture.** God has always been faithful; he cannot be otherwise (see Psalm 119:90). Even when we are faithless, he remains faithful—true to his Word, always fulfilling his promises (see 2 Timothy 2:13). The Bible is full of real-life stories that recount his trustworthy character. Read his Word. Write it down. Recite it to your heart. And when spiritual amnesia starts to set in, remember that God has a perfect track record of faithfulness.

2. **Cultivate faith in the midst of your feelings.** You won't always *feel* like God is faithful, but you can *know* deep in your heart that he will never fail. Train your mind to dwell on what is true, lovely, admirable, and praiseworthy (see Philippians 4:8-9). Take every wayward thought captive and make it obey Christ (see 2 Corinthians 10:4-5). While feelings are good indicators of what is happening inside us, they are not always trustworthy guides. God's truth always trumps feelings. Hebrews 11:1 reminds us, "Faith is the assurance of things hoped for, the conviction of things not seen." Faith gazes forward, not in fear, but in hope of the better land God has promised us—an eternal, unshakable Kingdom in heaven (see Hebrews 12:28).

3. **Focus on being faithful today.** Tomorrow is not ours to hold; today is what we have been given to steward (see Matthew 6:33-34). James offers this challenge: "Come now, you who say, 'Today or tomorrow we will go into such and such a town and spend a year there and trade and make a profit'—yet you do not know what tomorrow will bring. What is your life? For you are a mist that appears for a little time and then vanishes. Instead you ought to say, 'If the Lord wills, we will live and do this or that'" (James 4:13-15). By faith, we can leave the land of hypotheticals and live confidently, believing God's promises.

Don't forget: even though you don't know what tomorrow will bring, you know the God who will bring you through anything that comes your way.

Word before World
God is faithful, even when we are faithless.

Grow in Grace
Call to mind three ways God has been faithful in your life. Look forward in faith, knowing God will carry you through whatever you face.

62

LIFT YOUR EYES

I lift up my eyes to the hills. From where does my help come?
My help comes from the LORD, who made heaven and earth.

PSALM 121:1-2

A mother hangs her head low, her child's outright disobedience burdening her soul. She wonders, *What do I do now? Where does my help come from?*

A woman receives an email, her confidence stripped by the hurtful tirade of words. Tears fill her eyes as she stares at each accusation. She wonders, *How do I respond? Where does my help come from?*

A teenage girl looks down at the scale, the number she sees taunting her. She has restricted her diet and added extra workouts but she's starting to realize that even if she achieves the "right" number, it will never satiate her longing to be loved. She wonders, *How have I gotten here? Where does my help come from?*

As you read this book, I don't know what your day holds, what burdens you carry, or what responsibilities you have. But I do know that at some point today, tomorrow, or in the near future, your head will hang low and you'll wonder the same question: *Where does my help come from?*

Thousands of years ago, a fellow traveler on life's journey asked the same question. Psalm 121 is one of the Songs of Ascent. These psalms were intended to be sung by Jews on their journey to the Temple in Jerusalem at yearly festivals. While we know very little about this traveler, we can take comfort from this timeless prayer, which turns our aching hearts to our ever-present help in times of trouble (see Psalm 46:1).

As we journey over hills of heartache and through trenches of disappointment, seeking cover from the valley of the shadow of death (see Psalm 23:4), this psalm reminds us of one simple thing we need to do: lift our eyes from our troubles to the Lord, who provides us with the help we need.

Help does not come from within us; help comes from our Maker, who is with us (see Psalm 121:2).

When you lie awake, tossing and turning in the depths of the night, wondering what to say, what to do, and what will happen next, remember where your help comes from.

When exhaustion overwhelms you like the relentless summer sun, scorching your soul and preventing you from receiving much-needed rest, lift your eyes to God, who lifts his righteous right hand to shield you from the sun's heat.

God comes alongside us and lifts our eyes, our heads, and our hands so we can confidently say, "My help comes from the LORD, who made heaven and earth" (Psalm 121:2). The same God who guarded the writer of this psalm and those who sang its words on the way to Jerusalem guards you too. He watches over your life—not just in the daytime, but also in the nighttime. So lift your eyes from the messes around you, the worries that burden you, and the accusations that consume you, and receive help from your God, who never sleeps.

Word before World
Your help does not come from within; it comes
from the Lord, who is always with you.

Grow in Grace
Name what is ailing your soul today, and
then physically lift your eyes with confidence
in the Lord's provision and protection.

63

CATCHING FIREFLIES

O LORD, you have searched me and known me!
PSALM 139:1

During one week in late spring or early summer each year, a phenomenon happens below the treetops in the Great Smoky Mountains. Around the middle of May or June, after the sun goes down and the woods are hushed and shadowy, thousands of fireflies light up synchronously, like neon paint splattered between the trees. In order to actually see this glorious sight, you first have to win a lottery to receive entrance into the site. One year, Greg and I were fortunate enough to witness it in person.

If you manage to get a ticket, you park at a designated area on your slotted date, ride on a bus filled with strangers, hike a short trail into the heart of the mountains, and then wait for hours until the sun swaps places with the moon and you are surrounded by a cloak of darkness.

Then you pay careful attention, straining your eyes in the dark to spot a flash of light—even the smallest twinkle—hoping not to miss it. Then right before your eyes, tangled between bark and leafy branches, tiny glowing beetles light up together and then go dark. Light up, go dark—over and over.[1]

When I witnessed the synchronous fireflies, I held my breath, not wanting the moment to end. The bystanders stood crowded around us, hushed in collective awe. Oohs and aahs escaped our mouths. It's almost impossible to capture the beauty of the moment with a camera. Only an experienced photographer with a slow shutter can document this once-a-year miracle—you have to be there to truly grasp the wonder of it.

As captivating as this luminescent dance is, Psalm 139 records an even more captivating reality: the intimacy and nearness of God. David begins his prayer by recognizing that God knows every detail of his life and notices his sitting, standing, lying, and rising. He acknowledges God's sovereignty and his foreknowledge of the words that spill from his tongue. Suddenly, David is overcome with awe, and he confesses, "Such knowledge is too wonderful for me; it is high; I cannot attain it."

As David ponders God's nearness and knowledge, he is completely overwhelmed, amazed to the marrow of his bones. He realizes he could spend his entire life trying to grasp God's sovereignty and never come close, but he would try nonetheless. David knows that even if darkness covered him, the light of God's presence would still burst through the dark.

I once heard a missionary pose this question: "Are you watching for God? He's there." The same God who causes fireflies to light up simultaneously once a year in the Smokies is the same God who knows you intimately. He is with you when you sing at the top of your lungs on your commute to work. He knows how many hairs glide through the bristles of your brush. He sees you dab tears from your eyes after reading a moving story. He knows the thoughts that keep you awake at night, the words that slip from your tongue, the dreams that stir in your heart.

You don't have to go to a special place to see his movement or stand in awe of his majesty; you simply need to open his Word and look around you. Fix your mind on the wonderful, inconceivable thoughts of God, who pierces the darkness with the light of his Word, like fireflies lighting up the night.

Word before World
The Light of the World illuminates the
darkness of our world and our hearts.

Grow in Grace
Read Psalm 139:1-12 slowly, sifting each word through
your mind. Turn these words into a personal prayer to God.
Then go about your life and watch for God—
he's there with you, even in the darkness of the night.

64

CLOSE-UP MIRRORS

The one who looks into the perfect law, the law of liberty,
and perseveres, being no hearer who forgets
but a doer who acts, he will be blessed in his doing.

JAMES 1:25

I once made the terrible mistake of looking at my face in a magnifying mirror. Our family was staying in a hotel room where I discovered a retractable face mirror bolted to the bathroom wall. A ring of bright light glowed around the edge to help tired eyes like mine see clearly when applying makeup.

On one side was an ordinary mirror, while the other was capable of magnifying every pore, hair, vein, and flaw on my skin. When I turned the mirror to the magnifying side, I was *mortified*. I couldn't unsee my unkempt eyebrows (which looked fine to the naked eye) or gloss over my uneven complexion. I quickly flipped the mirror back to the other side and stared at the non-magnified version of my face, trying to forget the intimate details the close-up view had revealed.

James, an apostle and a half-brother of Jesus, explains in his letter that reading God's Word is like looking at our hearts in a close-up mirror. He writes, "Be doers of the word, and not hearers only, deceiving yourselves. For if anyone is a hearer of the word and not a doer, he is like a man who looks intently at his natural face in a mirror. For he looks at himself and goes away and at once forgets what he was like" (James 1:22-24).

Prior to James's admonition to be "doers of the word," he implores believers to put away wickedness and receive God's "implanted word" with meekness (verse 21). The person who commits to doing God's Word is the person whose heart has been pricked and softened by the gospel. This person receives the conviction that sprouts from God's Word and grows in grace through faithful obedience. The one who only hears God's Word is like a resistant child who ignores their parents when asked to clean their room—the words go in one ear and out the other.

Once we've seen the raw state of our souls and heard God's commands, we have a choice to make about how we will respond: with active obedience or with passive forgetting. Either we flip the mirror the other direction in a vain, self-gratifying attempt to forget our sins, or we walk away a new creation, clothed in righteousness, and ready to do good works in the name of Jesus.

Seeing ourselves accurately in light of God's perfect law yields a harvest in both the Kingdom of God and in our souls. So receive his Word with joy, and then be a doer of his Word.

May our lives reflect the image of Christ to the watching world.

Word before World
God's Word reveals who we really are and
invites us to be transformed into his image.

Grow in Grace
Meditate on James 1:26-27. How is God
calling you to be a doer of the Word?

65

THE OFFER OF YOUR KING

*Brothers and sisters, I do not consider myself yet to have taken
hold of it. But one thing I do: Forgetting what is behind
and straining toward what is ahead . . .*

PHILIPPIANS 3:13, NIV

There once was a girl who believed her ways were higher than her
King's. Each day she etched her plans into the cobblestones outside
his castle, hoping she could persuade him to make her dreams come true.

Her dainty hands grew calloused from etching the stubborn stone.
While she focused on the letters day after day, the King would visit her
and invite her into the castle for a delicious feast. But she didn't hear him
over the *scratch, scratch, scratch* of her carving knife against the rock.

The girl gathered treasures and, instead of enjoying them or thank-
ing the King for his provision, she stowed them in a safe place, believing
they would fit perfectly alongside the stone-carved plans she hoped would
come to pass.

As the years went by and her carvings grew deeper, the King continued to extend his invitation to dine with him in his castle. He wished she
would look up and behold the beauty around her and the life unfolding
before her eyes rather than being so consumed with writing her own
story.

One day, in her impatience with the King for not making her plans come
to fruition, her hand slipped, causing her to break her carving knife and

cut her hand. She threw away her treasures in a terrible fit and refused to go to the castle, choosing instead to remain at her cottage.

She was sulking with a bandaged hand when she heard a *tap-tap-tap* on the door. Opening it slowly, she found her King standing there with a bouquet of flowers and a picnic feast. She burst into tears at the generous, undeserved offer to her stubborn heart.

She took the King's arm, and they walked to the fields by the castle, laughing and dancing along the way. She gazed at eye-catching flowers she hadn't noticed before, her lungs breathed fresh air, and her ears heard the music of trees swaying in the wind.

In a flash, she realized that what she'd been given was better than what she longed for while etching her hopes and dreams in stone. Her plans paled in comparison to her King's love and presence.

She fretted over the wasted days, but the King is not one to look back. All along, he'd been etching a better story into her heart of stone—a story of surrender, a story of grace.

Word before World
God's ways and thoughts are higher, wider,
and deeper than our own.

Grow in Grace
What part of your story or plans are you holding
back from the Lord? Surrender your expectations
and accept God's offer to enjoy knowing him.

66

A TIME FOR EVERYTHING

There is a time for everything,
and a season for every activity under the heavens.
ECCLESIASTES 3:1, NIV

The yawns escaping my body feel deeper than the Mariana Trench—an unwelcome reminder of how incredibly exhausting this week has been. Life keeps speeding by without my consent. I'm reluctant to admit that I need rest, but I'm burned out, weary to the depths of my being. My Bible lies open in front of me, and every time I begin reading a verse, I stop midsentence to let out yet another whole-body yawn.

On days like these, I wonder how I can love God and have a flourishing walk with him when I can hardly read a verse without my body begging for rest. I am spiritually dry, and though the source of life is right before my eyes, I find myself glazing over with drowsiness.

Have you been there? Have you ever been so physically tired that it resulted in a time of spiritual dryness? Maybe you're in a season where waking up early to have alone time with God is nearly impossible, or maybe slowing down your schedule feels like a Herculean feat. You're spiritually thirsty, yet you can't seem to find time or energy to gulp down God's Word.

My oldest son has a habit of going the entire day without drinking a glass of water. By bedtime, he's dehydrated, and his body signals his need for water with a headache. This is the same son who balked at taking a nap when he was a toddler because he didn't want to miss out on any fun.

I used to remind him that he'd enjoy the day more if he rested; now I regularly remind him to make sure he's drinking—often placing a glass of cold water right in front of him.

King Solomon writes that there is a time for everything under the sun (see Ecclesiastes 3:1). Sometimes we need to take a nap instead of pressing forward. Sometimes we need to take a deep breath instead of hustling onward. Sometimes we need to let go of something we are clinging tightly to so we can receive more of Christ.

When we are spiritually dry from physical exhaustion, we may need to treat ourselves like a reluctant toddler and set everything aside for a brief time to take a nap or drink a big glass of water. We can close our eyes with our minds fixed on God, who keeps the world spinning when we are sleeping (see Psalm 121:4-5; Colossians 3:1-2).

There are times we need to stop what we're doing and take a couple of slow, deep breaths. Sometimes we need to ask for an hour of alone time so we can pray undistracted. We may need to shift our evening routine and go to bed earlier so we can wake up refreshed and ready to drink in God's Word.

Today, as my yawns keep escaping my mouth, instead of pressing on, I'm pressing pause so I can press into Jesus and the rest he gives. There is a time and season for everything; today, it's time to rest in my Savior. Will you join me?

Word before World
There is a time for everything, including taking a nap!

Grow in Grace
Growing in grace can be found by resting in
what Jesus has done for you and acknowledging
you need physical as well as spiritual rest.

IF . . .

So now faith, hope, and love abide, these three;
but the greatest of these is love.

1 CORINTHIANS 13:13

Imagine a church where the people are divided by loyalty to different leaders. They make excuses for their sinful actions and argue over unimportant issues. The people within this church are obsessed with outward displays of faith, but they neglect the deeper struggles in their hearts. They argue over how to gather, and they taint their theology with the world's teaching. Add all these descriptions up, and you get a glimpse into the church at Corinth—one of the churches the apostle Paul wrote letters to (1 and 2 Corinthians).

In 1 Corinthians 13, Paul goes straight to the heart of the matter, saying, "If I speak in the tongues of men and of angels, but have not love, I am a noisy gong or a clanging cymbal. And if I have prophetic powers, and understand all mysteries and all knowledge, and if I have all faith, so as to remove mountains, but have not love, I am nothing. If I give away all I have, and if I deliver up my body to be burned, but have not love, I gain nothing" (verses 1-3). Paul is basically saying, "If I do good things before people but I'm not fueled by the love of God, my actions are noisy, pointless, and fruitless."

I can't help but think about our own obsession with being seen, praised, and esteemed. In this technological era, we are more capable than ever of recording our achievements and good deeds before a wide audience in order to be seen and applauded. God's Word teaches us another way to sacrifice, love, and serve others—not out of a desire to be seen, but out of an overflow of love (see 1 Corinthians 16:14).

This question provides a good test for our actions: Are we sharing, serving, and doing good out of a love for God or a love for self? Here is my modern paraphrase of Paul's statements to the Corinthians:

If I share on social media, saying all the right things, but the love of Christ is not fueling my words, I am like a noisy gong and a clanging cymbal.

If I show up to serve at church only to be seen and praised by others, but I am not faithful in my everyday life, I am storing up treasures on earth, not in heaven.

If I judge my neighbor for doing the same things I do behind closed doors without repenting of my own sin, I am not living in the marvelous grace of Jesus.

But if I look to Christ, who embodies true sacrificial love, and if I forgive as I've been forgiven, the gospel will be proclaimed and Jesus will be glorified.

With the Holy Spirit's help, I can show genuine love to others—not because I am able, but because God is.

May we move toward Jesus, looking to his life and example. And may we follow in his footsteps, marked by love, sacrifice, forgiveness, and surrender.

Word before World
Love for Christ should fuel our every action (see 2 Corinthians 5:14).

Grow in Grace
Meditate on Paul's description of love in 1 Corinthians 13:3–8.
Pray for God's love to fuel your actions,
your sharing, your serving, and your motivation.

68

BUT GOD . . .

But God, being rich in mercy, because of the great love with
which he loved us, even when we were dead in our trespasses,
made us alive together with Christ—by grace you have been saved.

EPHESIANS 2:4-5

I could give you a million and one reasons why I'm not qualified to serve God. I could tell you about my past struggles—when an eating disorder almost took my life, when anxiety robbed me of peace, when at my lowest moment I wondered if death might be the only path to freedom from panic attacks, and when (on many occasions) I've doubted God's goodness.

I could easily recite my shortcomings because I know them all too well—and often rehearse them to myself. There's only one reason I don't harp on all my failures and won't stop using what God has given me for his glory. It's found in two small words in Paul's letter to the Ephesians: *but God*.

The gospel hinges on this conjunction. It is the door of hope swinging wide open, dispersing a burst of light that overcomes the darkness in our hearts. When put together, the phrase "but God" packs dynamite power capable of decimating the grip of past transgressions and stubborn strongholds, and silencing the deafening accusations of the enemy.

To summarize an earth-shattering, life-altering truth in the simplest way: the gospel of Jesus Christ changes *everything* about our past, our present, and our future. This truth is built on the foundation of the two words *but God*.

Theologian Timothy Keller writes, "The gospel is this: We are more sinful and flawed in ourselves than we ever dared believe, yet at the very same time we are more loved and accepted in Jesus Christ than we ever dared hope."[1] I did absolutely nothing to earn the love of God, and there is nothing I can do to lessen the gravity of his grace in Jesus Christ.

Ephesians 2:1–3 exposes the plight of every human being apart from Christ's redemptive work: "You were dead in the trespasses and sins in which you once walked, following the course of this world, following the prince of the power of the air, the spirit that is now at work in the sons of disobedience—among whom we all once lived in the passions of our flesh, carrying out the desires of the body and the mind, and were by nature children of wrath, like the rest of mankind."

Dead. Sons of disobedience. Children of wrath. This is who we were before God opened the door of hope through Christ's work on the cross. But this is no longer who we are—not because of anything we have done but because of what God has done through his Son, Jesus. "But God" changes everything.

But God, being rich in mercy . . .

But God, because of the great love with which he loved us . . .

But God, even when we were dead in our trespasses . . .

But God made us alive together with Christ—by grace you have been saved.

Salvation does not hinge on what we can or cannot accomplish. It does not hinge on our past sins or our present goodness. Salvation hinges on Christ's life, death, and resurrection. He gave his life to raise us from the dead.

"But God" changes everything—this is the good news of the gospel.

Word before World

Because of God's saving grace and steadfast love,
we are no longer defined by our past sins.

Grow in Grace

When you start to rehearse your sins, instead remember these
two words that are good news every single day: *but God.*

69

BUILD YOUR HOUSE

The wise woman builds her house, but with her own
hands the foolish one tears hers down.

PROVERBS 14:1, NIV

You are a builder. The question is not if you are building something but rather *what* you are building with your life.

Each day, you are building with your words, your ambition, your time, and your attention. You may not be creating a literal structure, but you are building your home, your work, and your relationships. Are you building walls or bridges, benches or barricades, shelters or shacks?

When my husband and I purchased our first home five years into our marriage, my initial instinct was to collect design ideas and gather inspiration for how our house would look. As I gathered images of homes unlike the one God had provided for us, my heart was seized with envy. Our cabinets were twenty years outdated, the floors were scuffed, the bathroom vanities had been purchased several seasons ago, and our hand-me-down furniture didn't match the newest styles.

Rather than seeing this earthly home as a gift to steward, I was laser-focused on what was lacking. I was building my home in discontentment instead of joy in the Lord.

King Solomon wrote, "The wise woman builds her house, but with her own hands the foolish one tears hers down" (Proverbs 14:1, NIV). Though

Solomon penned these words thousands of years ago, they hold true today. Women in King Solomon's time faced the temptation to tear apart what had been entrusted to them, just like we do today.

We are constantly peering into other people's lives through the internet, social media, and magazine racks at the grocery checkout. We see others' "houses"—their accomplishments, best moments, and touched-up photos—and we hyperfocus on all the ways our lives don't measure up. So we try in vain to build copycat lives while simultaneously tearing down what we've been given to steward.

Solomon explains that the wise woman builds her house while the foolish woman tears hers down. The key difference between the wise woman and the foolish woman is what she does with her hands. One woman builds her house because she fears the Lord and obeys his Word. The other woman tears down her house because she fears people and sets her hopes on being seen, applauded, and praised by others.

The wise woman follows Christ and builds her life on his Word— a foundation that can never be shaken. Christ is the embodiment of eternal wisdom, the heartbeat of the wise woman's life. When Christ put on flesh, he modeled what it looks like to build the Kingdom of God. He showed us that wisdom builds *bridges* that share the gospel. Wisdom builds *benches* that welcome others with hospitality and grace. Wisdom builds *shelters* that cover us and others with the promises of God's Word.

A wise woman uses encouraging words to build up those around her rather than tearing them down. She faithfully lays one brick at a time, looking to the future with hope (see Proverbs 31:25). Instead of building platforms, stages, profiles, and big dreams, a wise woman builds the Kingdom of God, which lasts forever.

Instead of winning friends, a wise woman makes disciples. Rather than obsessing over appearances, a wise woman cultivates a heart of worship. In place of gathering, hoarding, and coveting earthly treasures, a wise woman gives freely what she's freely received in Christ.

What will you build today?

Word before World

The wise woman builds bridges that share the gospel,
benches that welcome others in with hospitality, and
shelters that cover others with the promises of God's Word.

Grow in Grace

Take inventory of the life you are building.
What thoughts consume your mind?
What tasks fill up your days?
Build your life on Jesus Christ.

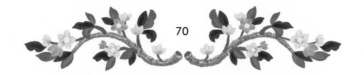

HOW TO WASTE YOUR LIFE
(A NONEXHAUSTIVE LIST)

Look carefully then how you walk, not as unwise but as wise,
making the best use of the time, because the days are evil.
Therefore do not be foolish, but understand what the will of the Lord is.

EPHESIANS 5:15-17

How to Waste Your Life

* View your behind-the-scenes responsibilities as unimportant.
* Allow anger to plant seeds of bitterness in your heart.
* Live for the praise of others.
* Delight in temporary fulfillment.
* Worry incessantly about what others think about you.
* Stress over your to-do list and unmet goals.
* Spend your days comparing yourself to others, competing with others, and criticizing those around you.
* Strive endlessly after perfection.
* Settle for half-hearted obedience to God.
* Build a platform for your fame.
* Obsess about creating a comfortable life.
* Always put yourself first.
* Complain and grumble when your schedule and plans change.
* Refuse to receive the gift of rest.
* Leave your Bible unopened, collecting dust on the bookshelf.
* Neglect meeting with the body of Christ.

✳ Want what you don't have.

✳ Keep what you do have.

✳ Quit what God has called you to do.

How Not *to Waste Your Life*

✳ Value your time with God above all else (see Psalm 73:25-26).

✳ Spend your days worshiping him in your ordinary, everyday life (see Colossians 3:23).

✳ Shape your days around God's Word (see Psalm 119:97).

✳ Rest in the finished work of Jesus (see Hebrews 4:11).

✳ Pray without ceasing, always giving thanks to God (see 1 Thessalonians 5:17).

✳ Love others the way Christ has loved you, and forgive as you've been forgiven (see Ephesians 4:32).

✳ Savor God's Word and hide it in your heart (see Psalm 119:11).

✳ Live with awe and wonder (see Psalm 8:1).

✳ Speak with grace and truth (see Colossians 4:6).

✳ Share the gospel with those around you (see Matthew 28:18-20).

✳ Embrace suffering as a means to knowing Christ more (see Philippians 3:10-11).

✳ Live from the overflow of your walk with God (see Colossians 2:6-7).

✳ Find more joy in giving than receiving (see Acts 20:35).

✳ Fear the Lord (see Proverbs 9:10).

✳ Faithfully gather with the body of Christ, and encourage others in the Lord (see Hebrews 10:25).

✳ Do justice, love mercy, and walk humbly with your God (see Micah 6:8).

✳ Care for the poor, the orphan, and the widow (see James 1:27).

✳ Walk as children of light (see Ephesians 5:8).

✳ Put on the whole armor of God and fight from the victory you have in Jesus (see Ephesians 6:10-20).

✳ Live for what matters eternally (see Matthew 6:19-21).

Word before World

Life is fleeting, but we can live for
what lasts into eternity, making the best use
of the time we are given each day.

Grow in Grace

What would you add to both of these lists?
Pray Ephesians 5:15-16, asking God
to guide your steps, fill you with wisdom,
and help you make the best use of the time.

71

EVEN WHEN YOU DON'T FEEL LIKE IT

I have set the LORD always before me;
because he is at my right hand, I shall not be shaken.

PSALM 16:8

There are seasons when I wake up and can't wait to open my Bible, and there are seasons when I leave it closed and reach for my phone instead. During times when I desire other things more than God, it is not because he has changed, it's because my desires have changed. Spending too much time focused on the things of this world weakens my love for God, causing me to crave what's fleeting instead of what's eternal.

Even in my wayward, half-hearted seasons, my faithless life does not nullify God's faithfulness (see 2 Timothy 2:13). C. S. Lewis writes of the predicament of choosing the world over the Word: "It would seem that Our Lord finds our desires not too strong, but too weak. We are half-hearted creatures, fooling about with drink and sex and ambition when infinite joy is offered us, like an ignorant child who wants to go on making mud pies in a slum because he cannot imagine what is meant by the offer of a holiday at the sea. We are far too easily pleased."[1]

I confess that I have been that child Lewis talks about—making mud pies in the slums, thinking this is as good as it gets when I could be delighting in the infinite riches of God's Word. But even when our desires are shallow, God takes our mediocre mudpies and trades them for his precious promises.

We can accept his invitation to enjoy a "holiday at the sea" and bask in the beauty of the gospel.

God's Word is filled with stories of people like us—frail, feeble, faltering, half-hearted creatures. At the same time, God's Word is jam-packed with glimpses into his faithful, consistent character. Like a multifaceted diamond, sparkling with perfect cuts, God reveals himself through the unfolding of his unfailing promises and his trustworthy nature. God is able to take our lack-luster desires and transform them into wholehearted affection for him. But in order to attune ourselves to his heart, we must come to him and open his Word.

There will always be obstacles we need to overcome in studying God's Word. Wayward feelings try to convince us that we don't need God. But he is greater than our feelings (see 1 John 3:20). Come to him in your brokenness, in your need, with your questions, with your apathetic desires. You may not *feel* like studying the Word, but you can know that life is found there, regardless of your feelings.

Bring every emotion and thought to the one who already knows them (see Psalm 139:1-3). Open your Bible, even when your desire is half-hearted and weak. As you set aside your mud pies and come to him, you'll experience full-ness of joy in his presence and enjoy pleasures forevermore (see Psalm 16:11). And these pleasures in Christ will be even better than a holiday at the sea.

Word before World

God is able to take our half-hearted desires
and fan them into whole-hearted love for him.

Grow in Grace

Don't let your feelings dictate whether you open God's
Word today. No matter how you're feeling, let your
emotions serve as a reminder that you need him.

72

THE FINGERPRINTS OF GOD

If you keep silent at this time, relief and deliverance
will rise for the Jews from another place, but you and
your father's house will perish. And who knows whether
you have not come to the kingdom for such a time as this?

ESTHER 4:14

Out of the sixty-six divinely inspired books of the Bible, only two don't mention God directly by name: Esther and Song of Solomon. Yet even in these two books where God's name is absent, his fingerprints are evident.

During a time when doubt shook the foundations of my faith, I ruminated on questions like these: *Does God really love me? What if my faith is all a sham? What if I wake up one day and find I've led people toward a hope that isn't real?*

The depth and uncertainty of those questions rattled me to the core. Even now, thinking about that season brings to the surface the pain and fear I experienced then. My confidence in God's presence in my life vanished, and every time I read the Bible, it felt like I was seeing his Word through a smudgy lens.

Around this time, I began studying the book of Esther. Like a detective, I combed through each verse, searching for God's fingerprints stamped within this book where he is not named.

This particular book is pivotal in biblical history, recording a time when the Israelites were almost wiped out. The book of Esther tells the story of an orphaned Jewish girl named Hadassah, or Esther, who became queen. God used Esther, along with her cousin Mordecai, who adopted her, to intercede boldly on behalf of the Israelites and save their people. In this life-and-death moment, God rescued his people through their radical obedience.

When we can't uncover his fingerprints in our circumstances, we can discover him in the Word.

God used the doubts that shook my faith as anchors to stabilize me in his truth. In his grace, he turned my eyes toward him and revealed his goodness, faithfulness, and steadfast love to me (see 1 Peter 1:8). The darkness I experienced made it possible for me to see the brightness of the Light again. I know doubts will resurface, but the book of Esther stands as a reminder to me of how he can be trusted to work behind the scenes today too.

If you are struggling to see God's fingerprints in the world, look for them in the Word. Read stories of how he has delivered his people in the past. The narrative of the Bible is not one of happenstance. Each book is intricately woven together in one grand display of God's glory and sovereignty. And when you can't seem to hold on to your faith, lean into friends who will pray for you and point you to Jesus.

God's name might not be mentioned in Esther, but his heart and handiwork are evident on every page. And take heart: his fingerprints are on every page of your story too.

Word before World
Even when God seems absent,
his fingerprints are present in your life.

Grow in Grace
What doubts are you facing right now?
Share those doubts with a trusted friend and ask them
to pray for you to see his fingerprints again soon.

73

DO NOT GROW WEARY

Let us not grow weary of doing good,
for in due season we will reap, if we do not give up.

GALATIANS 6:9

I've come to the point of burnout more times than I care to admit. You'd think I would have learned by now that I am a limited human being and there's only so far my body and mind can stretch until they break. Call it stubbornness, ignorance, or flat-out denial, but I still hold on to the belief that I can push past my limits and avoid the repercussions.

In Galatians 6:9, Paul encourages believers not to grow weary of doing good. In this passage, Paul is not advocating for a life of perpetual burnout but rather encouraging believers to persevere in the Lord and his strength.

Obedience to God does not mean we do *all* things; it means we do *all he has called us to do*—with his strength and for his glory. Paul urged the churches in Galatia not to lose heart or become discouraged as they lived in obedience to God's Word, doing good to everyone, especially those in the household of faith (verse 10).

As Christians, we are saved through faith alone by grace, but the evidence of our faith is our works (see Ephesians 2:8-9; James 2:26). When the love and grace of Christ changes our hearts, our actions are also transformed (see Ephesians 2:10). And yet, when we do not see the harvest for the work we are doing, weariness has a way of setting in. We may even teeter on the brink of burnout as we sow gospel seeds and sacrifice for others. This is when Paul takes us by the hand and exhorts us not to give up, reminding us that the harvest will come in God's perfect timing.

I love Galatians 6:11, where Paul writes, "See with what large letters I am writing to you with my own hand." In Paul's day, the custom was for the letter writer to dictate his words to a scribe. Instead of having someone else write these final words, Paul wrote them himself—and he did so in a larger font. Paul knew firsthand the weariness we will face as we live for Christ. He faced the same temptation to lose heart when waiting for gospel seeds to sprout. Yet he also knew the harvest was coming and placed his hope in God!

It's easy to lose heart in a world of instant gratification. Following Christ requires patience, perseverance, and eternal perspective. Weariness will come, but we can keep our eyes on Jesus, who persevered to the end.

* In your involvement in your church, *do not lose heart.*
* As you disciple the children in your life, *do not lose heart.*
* In praying for the lost, *do not lose heart.*
* As you lay down your desires to serve others, *do not lose heart.*
* In declaring the good news of Jesus Christ, *do not lose heart.*

We do not lose heart because we serve a risen Savior who supplies us with all we need to do what he has called us to do (see 2 Corinthians 9:8; Philippians 4:19). He has not called us to do everything—we are simply called to be faithful and to rest in him. He refreshes our weary souls, and he brings the harvest in due time. So keep going, keep giving, and keep serving—in his strength and for his glory.

Word before World

When weariness sets in, remember Christ,
who persevered to the very end and who supplies
us with the strength we need to continue doing
the good works he has called us to do in his name.

Grow in Grace

Have you grown weary of doing good?
Evaluate the areas in your life where you feel like giving up.
What is the source of your discouragement?
If God has called you to it, press on in faith,
knowing the harvest is coming.

WHERE JOY IS FOUND

These things I have spoken to you,
that my joy may be in you, and that your joy may be full.

JOHN 15:11

Have you lost your joy lately, and you're not sure where to find it? If so, you're not alone—I have been there more times than I can count. When my schedule is packed to the brim, I often find myself joyless as I try to keep up with an impossible pace. Not long ago, the stress of work along with managing the schedules and needs of my three children brought me to the brink of exhaustion. My time with Jesus fell by the wayside, and I almost skipped the local Bible study I attend each Wednesday. I knew from past experience, though, that my joy in Jesus is renewed when I spend time with sisters in Christ. So I went anyway, and even though my body was tired, my soul was refreshed as we read God's Word together.

If we truly want heart change, we have to go to the one who changes hearts.

But what does this actually look like? How do we spend time with Jesus when we can't see or touch him?

Though we can't touch, see, and talk to Jesus in person, God has provided ways for us to commune with him while we wait for his return. Here are some tangible ways to spend time with him—and retrieve our joy.

* **Spend time with Jesus by fellowshiping with his body, the local church.** We grow in godliness by spending time with his people. It's possible to have nothing else in common with someone, but when you both have Christ, you can form the greatest bond of fellowship. God has given us brothers and sisters in Christ to encourage and be encouraged by, to worship with, and to learn from and alongside (see Acts 4:32). When we spend time with other believers, we are spending time with our Savior.

* **Spend time with Jesus by reading (or listening to) the Word.** Jesus is the embodiment of the Word of God. John writes, "The Word became flesh and dwelt among us, and we have seen his glory, glory as of the only Son from the Father, full of grace and truth" (John 1:14). We can't know Christ intimately apart from the Word, because every page of Scripture points to him (see Luke 24:27).

* **Spend time with Jesus by enjoying his creation.** Colossians 1:16 says, "By him all things were created, in heaven and on earth, visible and invisible, whether thrones or dominions or rulers or authorities—all things were created through him and for him." Creation shouts his glory (see Psalm 19:1). We can spend time with Jesus by enjoying the world he has made.

* **Spend time with Jesus through worship.** Turn on worship music and sing a song of praise. You might want to physically get on your knees in a posture of humility and pray through a psalm. Talk to him by praying his Word and singing his praises (see Psalm 95:1-3; Ephesians 5:19).

* **Spend time with Jesus by loving your nieghbors (including your children, your spouse, your friends, and your coworkers).** Jesus explained that the greatest commandment is to love the Lord with all your heart, soul, and mind, and the second is to "love your neighbor as yourself'" (Matthew 22:36-40). One way we love Jesus is by loving the people around us, following his example of humility and sacrifice (see John 15:12-17).

✳ **Spend time with Jesus by feeding the hungry, giving to the poor, and caring for those in need.** In Matthew 25:40-45, Jesus tells about the final judgment, shedding light on how we can serve him by serving "the least of these." We spend time with Jesus by giving to those in need, knowing when we serve and give to others in his name, we do it for him.

Spending time with Jesus might look like getting away and being alone with him, but it might also look like being with others who point you to him. His presence is with us, and his Word is alive and gives life to our souls. This is the path to true, soul-satisfying joy.

Word before World

Joy is found in spending time with Christ,
the ultimate source of joy.

Grow in Grace

Whatever it takes, set aside some time to
spend with Jesus today. Right where you are,
with what you have, make your life about him,
around him, for him, and through him.

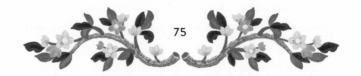

75

TUNE YOUR HEART

My heart is steadfast, O God, my heart is steadfast!
I will sing and make melody!
PSALM 57:7

If the thoughts of your heart were a melody, what tune would they play? Would the notes be out of tune, filled with complaining and grumbling? Would they be ominous, resounding with fear and dread? Would they be dissonant, booming with anger and bitterness? Or would a harmony of gratitude and thanksgiving flow from the reverberations of your soul?

What we read, listen to, watch, and pay attention to (input) directly impacts our actions, attitudes, worldview, and judgments (output). In other words, if we were to strike a guitar string with a pinecone instead of a guitar pick, we'd hear sounds we don't desire. Likewise, what we meditate on, mull over, and think about produces either notes of peace and praise in our hearts or notes of discord and discontentment.

Some days my soul is completely out of tune with God. When I wake up and tune in to the news first thing, it strikes a note of fear that reverberates through the rest of the day. Often, I don't even realize the chord has been struck until later, when I'm quick tempered and on edge.

When we become more attuned to the clamors of the world over God's Word, our hearts become out of tune with him.

While David was hiding from King Saul in a cave, he penned a psalm of praise to God. In the middle of his mess, when his soul was "in the midst of lions," he could have easily complained or cowered in fear. Instead, David sang a song: "My heart is steadfast, O God, my heart is steadfast! I will sing and make melody! Awake, my glory! Awake, O harp and lyre! I will awake the dawn! I will give thanks to you, O Lord, among the peoples; I will sing praises to you among the nations. For your steadfast love is great to the heavens, your faithfulness to the clouds" (Psalm 57:7-10).

When you're stuck in the middle of a stressful situation and you see no way out, tune your heart to sing praise to God. He is merciful to those who seek him, a refuge for those in need of shelter. He fulfills his purpose for us, and he tramples our enemies (see Psalm 138:7-8). We can strike a note of confident praise to the Lord by reminding our souls of his steadfast love and faithfulness (see Psalm 57:3).

Even when we are hiding in a cave of fear, God is still exalted above the heavens. Even when our mouths are glued shut, he is still worthy to be praised. As the hymn writer Robert Robinson describes, God's streams of mercy are never ceasing and call for our songs of loudest praise.[1] We can tune our hearts to sing his grace by inputting gospel truth into our souls. The hope of God's Word will compose a melody in us that reverberates for all eternity.

Word before World
A heart tuned to the words and wisdom
of God produces a melody of praise.

Grow in Grace
Turn on your favorite worship music
today and sing praises to God!

76

FULLY LOVED, FULLY FREE

If the Son sets you free,
you will be free indeed.

JOHN 8:36

ave you ever wanted to hide your brokenness from others so much that it kept you from experiencing true fellowship?

Me, too.

I once almost missed out on a trip with friends simply because I didn't want them to see my vulnerable, hurting heart. Though I knew these women from our interactions online, I had never met them in person, and we were going on a trip to get to know one another. The timing of the trip could not have been worse. I was running on fumes, trying to finish work projects, manage our home, and care for our children. From the outside, I assumed these women all had their lives together, and I feared being exposed as a fraud. *What if I cry in front of my new friends? What if I fall apart in front of these women I deeply respect and have been inspired by? What if I panic being away from home and embarrass myself?* These what-if questions swirled in my mind like a tornado.

By God's grace, I went anyway, lugging along my brokenness and extra baggage but also the promises of God. And you know what? Each of those what-if fears came to fruition.

I *did* cry.

I *did* fall apart.

I *did* struggle with panic.

And my new friends still loved me like Jesus does.

God used these friends to show me that his love for me does not decrease in my lowest moments or increase in my mountaintop moments. His love is complete, fulfilled—a done deal through Christ.

Fully loved, fully free, fully his: this is who I am, and this is who you are too.

Satan tempts us to hide our brokenness by plastering on an "I'm fine" smile while we bleed inside. Just as Adam and Eve sewed fig leaves together in an attempt to hide their transgression, we try to hide from God and the people he has placed around us. We sweep our struggles under the rug, mask our pain with platitudes, and tidy up our anxiety by acting as if we are invincible, as if we can hide our need for help.

But Jesus did not come for those who have their act together; he came for the hurting, the broken, and the needy (see Luke 5:31-32). He came to set us free, eliminate the need for our fig leaves, and cloak us with a better covering—his shed blood (see Ephesians 1:7; 1 John 1:7).

Gospel-centered friendship is not rooted in showing off our independence or our ability to control the details of our lives; it is found in showing up just as we are, seeking Christ in the middle of our brokenness. Godly friendship flourishes when we speak words of life into weary souls—and when we receive those words ourselves.

Breakdowns often lead to breakthroughs, which God uses to break apart the lies and strongholds gripping us. We weren't made to walk alone. But we must be willing to start walking broken, knowing Jesus is with us and trusting that he loves us every step of the way as we follow him.

Will you risk loving someone else that way? And will you risk being loved that way?

Word before World

Fully loved, fully free, fully his—
this is who you are in Christ!

Grow in Grace

What brokenness or struggle are you
attempting to hide from God and others?
Ask God to set you free so you can hear
and speak words of life today.

77

THE SECRET IS THIS

I can do everything through Christ,
who gives me strength.

PHILIPPIANS 4:13, NLT

o you want to know the secret to a life of contentment?

Here's a hint: contentment is not found in getting rid of all your things and living a minimalist lifestyle. It's not found in surpassing milestones, meeting big goals, or having a nicer home. It's not found in focusing on the present moment or breathing deeply. While there is nothing wrong with those things, if they're devoid of Christ, they won't lead to lasting contentment. It is possible to get rid of all your possessions, simplify your life, reach your goals, practice a mindful life, and still battle discontentment.

With chains bruising his wrists, the apostle Paul shared how he learned the secret to contentment: "Not that I am speaking of being in need, for I have learned in whatever situation I am to be content. I know how to be brought low, and I know how to abound. In any and every circumstance, I have learned the secret of facing plenty and hunger, abundance and need. I can do all things through him who strengthens me" (Philippians 4:11-13).

Paul makes it crystal clear that the secret to contentment is not found in what *I* do . . . the secret is *through Christ*, who gives me strength. As Elisabeth Elliot once said, "The secret is Christ in me, not me in a different set of circumstances."[1]

Contentment is possible when our hope is deeply rooted in Christ, who faced every temptation and struggle we face, yet was without sin. If Paul could learn contentment while confined to a prison cell, we can learn contentment too, no matter what challenges we're up against.

This includes when your friends are getting married, and you are still single. When other couples are having children, and you remain childless. When everyone around you is healthy, and you're facing chronic illness. When others' lives appear to be easy, and your family is facing an unexpected trial. When your bank account is low, and bills still need to be paid. Even when things are going well, just the way you hoped. No matter the situation, the path to contentment is the same: fixing our eyes on Christ.

Jesus is the answer to your needs and longings. He is the giver of strength, the author of faith, and the source of lasting joy. When our contentment hinges not on circumstances lining up with our plans but on Christ, who is the fulfillment of God's promises, we find strength to accept our reality and rejoice with those around us. We can enjoy eternal perspective as we live in the present moment with our gaze on the joy to come.

The secret to contentment is found not in having more or having less; it's found in having Christ.

Word before World
When Christ is the source of our contentment,
no circumstance, trial, emotion,
or situation can strip us of our joy.

Grow in Grace
Identify an area where you are battling discontentment.
How does knowing that Christ is with you
and in you transform your perspective?

78

BREATHE OUT WORRY

When I said, "My foot is slipping," your unfailing love,
LORD, supported me. When anxiety was great within me,
your consolation brought me joy.

PSALM 94:18-19, NIV

Sometimes as I lie in my bed, an onslaught of thoughts and worries barrages my mind like water over a broken dam. These thoughts rush through without caution, and it's impossible to catch or contain them. When my mind is running full steam ahead, it doesn't matter how tired my body is—I'm wide awake under the deluge.

I am desperate for rest, but instead I'm tossed on unrelenting waves of worry. I try to pray, only to find myself without words. Sometimes all I can do is attempt to slow my breathing and focus on the Lord.

Martin Luther described prayer this way: "To be a Christian without prayer is no more possible than to be alive without breathing."[1] Prayer is the respiration of a Christian—the release of toxic worry and the intake of God's life-giving, undeserved mercy. Prayer is our lifeline; it's oxygen to our souls, supplying us with life and vitality. Just as breathing enables our entire bodies to function properly, prayer enables our spiritual lungs to inhale God's promises.

One way to rest in God's presence during times of worry is to breathe slowly and deeply, to be still and know that he is God, even when the waters rage all around us. When we take a deep breath, pray, and harness the worries swirling in our minds with the help of the Holy Spirit, God will show us a deeper, fuller, more lasting response to anxiety.

When God created Adam in the Garden of Eden, he breathed into his soul, giving him the breath of life (see Genesis 2:7). God created the world by speaking, but he gave life to Adam with his very breath.

God still breathes into us through the indwelling Holy Spirit as we read his living and active Word (see Hebrews 4:12). To read and pray God's Word is to breathe again spiritually. When the dam of worry breaks and thoughts flood our souls, he invites us to meet with him—and in doing so, to climb aboard the rescue boat of mercy.

There will still be nights when the dam of worry breaks. But God's grace is sufficient; his mercy is our anchor in the storm. He is still breathing life into our souls through the hope of his Word. Deep breaths remind us to slow down and remember his unfailing mercy. We have something better than simply emptying our minds of worry; we have the opportunity to fill ourselves with the knowledge of his presence.

When we breathe in his mercy and breathe out our worry, our lungs can fill with genuine praise.

Word before World

Prayer slows us down so we can rest in Christ in a
restless world. When we are consumed by worry,
we can breathe in his mercy, like oxygen for our souls.

Grow in Grace

The next time you find yourself lying in bed, unable to sleep,
try inhaling God's mercy for a count of five and then
exhaling your worry for a count of five. Then rest in
God's sovereignty and sleep in His embrace.

79

NOTHING LESS

Together, we are his house, built on the foundation of the apostles
and the prophets. And the cornerstone is Christ Jesus himself.

EPHESIANS 2:20, NLT

I am standing in church, singing with the congregation as we worship together. The lyrics to "My Hope Is Built on Nothing Less" appear on the screen, and as soon as the song begins, I sense a noticeable difference in the congregation. People of all ages and backgrounds join in singing these words that reach the depths of the human heart:

> *My hope is built on nothing less*
> > *than Jesus Christ, my righteousness*
> *I dare not trust the sweetest frame*
> > *but wholly lean on Jesus' name*[1]

This song was penned by an imperfect person like me who came to understand that everything crumbles when we do not build our hope on Christ or do not center our souls on him.

The guitarist plays and we continue singing:

> *On Christ the solid Rock, I stand*
> > *All other ground is sinking sand*
> > *All other ground is sinking sand*

As I sing, I think about all the ways I live contrary to these words. I act as if my hope is dependent on what I am capable of doing—or not doing. I say my hope is built on nothing less than Jesus' blood and righteousness, but I shatter when I don't get my way or when my home is a constant mess or when I can't keep up with my to-do list or when things I want to control slip through my fingers.

We've all been there. Something difficult happens, and we realize we've built our hope on sinking sand. We lash out in anger toward someone who disagrees with us, harbor resentment when we're hurt by a friend, and berate the body God has given us, frustrated that it doesn't look the way we want it to.

We build our hope on our accomplishments, our comfort, our appearance, our health, and what we think we can control. When we build our hope on anything besides Jesus, we crumble at the first tremor of an earthquake.

> *When darkness veils his lovely face*
> *I rest on his unchanging grace*
> *In every high and stormy gale*
> *My anchor holds within the veil*

We often have to endure hardship to realize this truth. It's only when we have nothing left on this earth and are left with Christ alone that we realize we have everything we could need in him.

Eternal hope is not built on our abilities but on the hidden wisdom of God, revealed to us in Jesus (see 1 Corinthians 2:7). We join Paul and proclaim the gospel of Christ—in our weakness, in our trembling, and in our fear. We proclaim the gospel as we face our personal shortcomings, because the power to save is found not within us but in God.

The music swells as the congregation sings the last chorus, declaring one more time,

On Christ the solid Rock, I stand
  All other ground is sinking sand
  All other ground is sinking sand

The foundation for our hope is nothing more and nothing less than Jesus' blood and righteousness. Christ's atoning sacrifice is sufficient. His provision of grace for us day by day is sufficient. We stand on him who is sovereign over every leaf that falls, every speck of dust that swirls through the air, every moment that unfolds in history. We stand on his perfect life and sacrifice, which covers our sins and sets us free from the shackles of shame we lug around with us. We stand on him who gives us power to persevere as we face persecution.

Our hope is built on Jesus Christ, whose Kingdom stands forever.

Word before World
On Christ the solid Rock we stand;
all other ground is sinking sand.

Grow in Grace
What holds you back from building your
life on Jesus' blood and righteousness?
Join Paul in proclaiming your freedom in Christ alone.

JESUS LOVES YOU EVEN IN THE MOMENTS YOU DON'T HAVE YOUR ACT TOGETHER

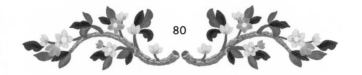

80

UNEXPECTED DELIVERANCE

God heard their groaning, and God remembered his
covenant with Abraham, with Isaac, and with Jacob.
God saw the people of Israel—and God knew.

EXODUS 2:24-25

"Now there arose a new king over Egypt, who did not know Joseph"
(Exodus 1:8). The book of Exodus begins on a dismal note—as if
an ominous "da da da dun" were playing in the background. Following the
grand finale to the book of Genesis, where the Israelites were flourishing
in the land of Egypt under Joseph's leadership, Exodus opens with an era
of oppression under a new king.

After Joseph, his brothers, and the rest of their generation died in
Egypt, the Israelites increased in number and strength (see Exodus 1:7).
The new king of Egypt saw the Israelites as a threat to their land and to
his authority, so he imposed heavy burdens on them. Despite the yoke
of slavery around their necks, God's people continued to multiply (see
verse 12).

In another attempt to quell the Israelites' flourishing, the king
of Egypt commanded the Hebrew midwives to put to death every
son born to the Hebrew women (see verse 16). Driven by their fear
of Yahweh rather than Pharaoh, the midwives spared the baby boys,
claiming that Hebrew women gave birth too quickly (see verse 19). So
Pharaoh took his heinous plan to stop the Hebrews from multiplying a

step further and demanded that the sons be cast into the Nile River (see verse 22).

The Exodus narrative zooms in on the story of a Hebrew woman who feared God. In Exodus 2, we learn that this woman gave birth to a son, hid him for three months, and then set him in a basket in the Nile. Later in the book of Exodus, we find out that her name is Jochebed, the mother of Moses (see Exodus 6:20).

Can you imagine how Jochebed must have felt in this moment? With her hands shaking and her heart beating wildly, she placed her beloved child in the reeds of the Nile, putting her hope in the God of Israel for miraculous deliverance. Not long after Jochebed's surrender of her son, Moses was rescued from the reeds by Pharaoh's daughter and eventually brought into the royal household (see Exodus 2:5-6).

The Hebrew word for "basket" also means ark. It's the same word used in Genesis 7 to refer to Noah's ark.[1] Two different times in the Old Testament, God used an ark as a means of salvation for his people—through a boat for Noah and his family and through a basket for a Hebrew baby who would one day lead the Israelites out of Egyptian slavery. These were foreshadowings of the ultimate deliverance that came to us through a Baby born in humble means in the unimpressive town of Bethlehem (see Matthew 2:1-12). All three times, God's deliverance came in unexpected ways, right on time (see Galatians 4:4).

In your longing for deliverance from whatever you are facing, do not be disillusioned if deliverance does not come how—or when—you expect. Life is hard, but God is faithful. Life is full of dead ends and detours, but God sees them coming.

You may be looking for a way out from under the crushing defeat of whatever is oppressing you, but instead God may give you an ark—an unexpected vessel to keep you afloat. When tough times come, hang on tight to him.

Word before World

Deliverance may not come in the way we expect,
but we can take heart that deliverance
has already come in Christ.

Grow in Grace

Think back on some times in your life
when you needed deliverance.
What arks did God provide?

81

WHATEVER

*Whatever you do, in word or deed, do everything in the name of
the Lord Jesus, giving thanks to God the Father through him.*

COLOSSIANS 3:17

There's probably a woman out there who loves folding laundry and scrubbing dirty dishes, but I am not that woman. I don't naturally love cleaning and picking up *every single day*. With five people under one roof, our home gets messy faster than a dog goes after a bone. Sometimes it feels like food and toys get strewn across the floor the moment I finish picking up and vacuuming!

Why do I even clean? I often grumble to myself. *It's just going to get messy in another minute.*

It may feel like an exercise in futility, but there's a reason for doing these mundane tasks—one that's deeper than having a spotless home. It's all about a little word in Colossians 3:17 and 23: *whatever*.

In this passage, Paul is writing to the church at Colossae, instructing them in the glorious ways of Christ. He begins his letter by laying out why Christ is worthy of all praise (see Colossians 1:13-22). Then he tells them specific ways they can practically live for God's glory since they have "put off" the old self and "put on" their new self in Christ (Colossians 3:9-10).

We are to get dressed in the gospel each day and preach this awe-inspiring truth to our hearts: "Christ is all, and in all" (Colossians 3:11). Paul goes on to say, "*Whatever* you do, in word or deed, do *everything* in the name of the Lord Jesus, giving thanks to God the Father through him" (verse 17, emphasis added). This is a lofty calling. Could he really mean that?

Whatever includes everything. It includes doing the dishes, and it includes picking up toys for the thousandth time. It includes folding countless loads of laundry every week, and it includes vacuuming, grocery shopping, and being a shuttle service. It includes responding to emails, driving in traffic, and dealing with difficult coworkers. This little word *whatever* not only redeems the time spent doing the mundane tasks of life but also gives us greater purpose and joy in doing them. If we look at daily housework, errands, and assignments simply as chores to be completed, we will miss out on something glorious: knowing Jesus better through them.

Worship isn't just relegated to Sunday morning church or a daily quiet time. Worship is adoring Jesus every moment of the day, including the moments when we're doing tasks we don't necessarily love to do.

Even the mundane moments of life have meaning and purpose. No task is exempt from the holy call of doing everything for the glory of God. Jesus makes your "whatever" worthwhile.

The unfiltered, unfancy moments of life are made beautiful when we recognize that God's fingerprints are all over these minuscule moments. We just need eyes to see him at work all around us and within us.

The key to finding joy and purpose in the mundane is to remember the call of "whatever" and to do everything with Jesus and for him. Paying bills, cleaning out the car, inputting data into a spreadsheet all become joy-filled worship when done to the glory of God. Scrubbing dishes is redeemed when we praise him as we clean each dish.

He can redeem every chore on your agenda today—even that umpteenth load of laundry.

Word before World
Even the most mundane tasks
can become sweet times of worship
when done for the glory of God.

Grow in Grace
Whatever you are doing today, whether it's ironing shirts,
folding laundry, cleaning, punching the clock,
or chasing little ones, do it for the Lord. The next time
you find yourself grumbling about a mindless task,
picture Jesus meeting you in that mundane moment.

82

MINDFUL OF GOD

When I look at your heavens, the work of your fingers,
the moon and the stars, which you have set in place,
what is man that you are mindful of him, and
the son of man that you care for him?

PSALM 8:3-4

For years, I've searched for a quick fix to anxiety. When it comes to suffering and sanctification, my flesh yearns for the easy way out. I'd prefer to travel on a paved road fringed with wildflowers, convenient refreshment stands, and rest stops every few miles. But this is not what the road before us looks like most of the time. The path of life is often unpaved, winding, and difficult to navigate.

Paul described suffering as an opportunity to know Christ and the power of his resurrection. He saw his trials as a chance to share in Christ's sufferings and to become like him in his death (see Philippians 3:10). Amy Carmichael likewise described suffering as a chance to die, the gateway to abundant life.[1]

There is no shortcut when it comes to sharing in the sufferings of Christ, and this is true when we face anxiety.

If you were to do an internet search for antidotes to anxiety, you'd quickly come across the concept of mindfulness. While this idea holds merit in terms of reminding us to focus on the present rather than worry about the future, it falls short when it comes to reminding us who we can release our worries to: our Maker and Sustainer. As we traverse the bumpy roads of life, wandering through desert wastelands and winding along mountainous heights, anxiety often tailgates close behind. We fear what might happen and obsess over what's just beyond the horizon. Being mindful of God brings our focus back to our Creator, who loves us, knows the way we take, and carries us through.

King David was so overcome with the majesty of God that he exclaimed, "O Lᴏʀᴅ, our Lord, how majestic is your name in all the earth!" (Psalm 8:9). David was dumbfounded by the reality of God's generous care for his people. Awe of God led David to wonder, "When I look at your heavens, the work of your fingers, the moon and the stars, which you have set in place, what is man that you are mindful of him, and the son of man that you care for him?" (Psalm 8:3-4) David was mindful of God, and he was blown away by the reality that God is mindful of him.

Christian mindfulness leads us to greater awe of God, not the emptiness of our minds. It opens our eyes to see God's handiwork around us and within our hearts, shaping our thoughts to be centered around his grace, not our mistakes and shortcomings.

Are we more mindful of what we fear in the future than we are of the God who sent his Son to die in our place? Are our minds so preoccupied with what might be beyond the horizon that we are missing out on the good things God is unfolding right before our eyes?

Raise your gaze to the heavens, and admire God's handiwork (see Psalm 19:1). Enjoy fellowship with him through prayer as you navigate life's twists and turns, and find relief from the pangs of anxiety by filling your mind full of his truth. He is inviting you to be mindful of him—the one who is always mindful of you.

Word before World

Being mindful of God brings our thoughts back to the one who holds us, walks with us, and sustains us as we travel the winding paths before us.

Grow in Grace

How can you be mindful of God today? Make it your aim to center your thoughts around God's glory, majesty, and care as you go through your day.

83

IN THE BLINK OF AN EYE

For all have sinned and fall short of the glory of God,
and are justified by his grace as a gift,
through the redemption that is in Christ Jesus.

ROMANS 3:23-24

It happens in the blink of an eye. Our gaze shifts from what God has given us to what he has given someone else, and we start to covet what they have. We glance in the other direction when slandering our neighbor and then brush it off as a joke. We click a button, and it leads us down a rabbit hole to a destructive habit.

Patterns of sin can be blatantly obvious at times, and other times they can be as inconspicuous as a chameleon. Jesus said it clearly: it is possible to appear righteous while having a heart still entrenched in sin (see Matthew 23:28).

We live in a world that's obsessed with outward appearances. Simply scroll social media or spend a few minutes online, and you'll be bombarded by ads to help you lose weight, burn fat, or get a flat tummy in just seven minutes a day. You'll find life hacks for all your organizational woes and regular reminders of all you need to do to get your home and wardrobe up to date.

When Jesus confronted the Pharisees over their sin, he did not address their outward obedience. His concern was their inward pride. These men of the law were outwardly obsessed with appearing righteous, yet their hearts were not aligned with God. In the words of Jesus, they were "blind guides," "whitewashed tombs," "hypocrites"—"full of dead people's bones and all uncleanness" (Matthew 23:24-27). On the outside, the Pharisees were put-together spiritual giants, but at their core, they were dead. Jesus regularly spoke against the Pharisee's love of the law, because in their love for being right, they got it all wrong. They did not see how the law pointed to and was fulfilled by Jesus (see Matthew 5:17-20).

So what does this mean for us as we battle the temptation to display outward acts of righteousness instead of full-fledged commitment to Christ? We must go back to the heart.

Our motives make or break us—they reveal where our allegiance is rooted. We may do the same action but for different reasons. We might serve at church, give to the poor, or make a meal in order to be seen, or we might do those same things quietly out of sincere love for God and his people and for his Kingdom. Only we—and God—know the motivation of our hearts, and only he can purify our motives.

God can transform not only our actions but also our motivations. Because of Christ, we are no longer defined by our shortcomings; our scarlet sins are washed white as snow by his shed blood (see Isaiah 1:18). We walk in grace, turning our gaze back to him who cleanses us from the inside out.

When we come to him, leaving behind hypocrisy and embracing repentance, we are forgiven and set free—in the blink of an eye.

Word before World
Because of Christ, our scarlet sins are
washed white as snow by his shed blood.

Grow in Grace
In what areas of your life are you attempting to cover up sinful
heart motivations with outward good works? God sees your heart
and desires whole-hearted obedience. Fix your eyes on Christ,
repent of your sin, receive his forgiveness, and walk in his grace.

84

THE SECRET LIFE OF A CHRIST-FOLLOWER

Your Father who sees in secret will reward you.

MATTHEW 6:18

The secret life of a Christ-follower is not one of duplicity; it is one of simplicity—serving, giving, praying, and fasting in secret to know God more.

Sandwiched in the Sermon on the Mount is Jesus' warning to his followers: "Beware of practicing your righteousness before other people in order to be seen by them, for then you will have no reward from your Father who is in heaven" (Matthew 6:1). Every time I read this passage I cringe, because I know how tempting it is to do good for God with the hope that others will see what I'm doing and praise my righteousness.

This happens when we do things like this:

* Hold the offering plate in a way that lets other people see how much we are giving.
* Post about a mission project we participated in so we'll be praised for our sacrifice.
* Raise our hands in worship, not out of reverence and love for God but to appear holy.
* Fast from food (or something else) and make sure everyone knows about it.
* Pray in a way that people will notice our flamboyant words while we neglect to pray in secret.

How many times have we received the fleeting reward of being praised by others and missed the joy of deep intimacy with God? Jesus makes it clear in his sermon that our Father sees what we do in secret and will reward us in eternity.

Who we are behind closed doors reveals what we really believe about God. Do we treasure an intimate walk with our Maker? Or do we value the praise of those around us? What's done in secret never remains in secret; it forms who we are and impacts how we live.

The secret life of a Christ-follower is one of authentic faith and love for God. We give cheerfully to God, who has supplied us with grace upon grace (see 2 Corinthians 9:7). We pray without ceasing, giving thanks to God, submitting our requests to him, and acknowledging his lordship over our lives (see Matthew 6:8-14; 1 Thessalonians 5:17-18). We fast, laying aside food or pleasures we have become dependent on, in order to seek the fullness of God (see Matthew 6:16-17).

Do not underestimate time spent in secret with God, money given in secret in the name of Jesus, fasting done in secret to acknowledge our dependence on him, and prayers whispered in secret as we submit our will to his. The secret life of a Christ-follower is the springboard for joy and fullness on earth as we await the treasure of being with him in heaven.

Psalm 73:25 says, "Whom have I in heaven but you? And there is nothing on earth that I desire besides you." The greatest reward we could ever receive is not to be praised by the lips of others but to be near God and to praise his holy name.

Word before World

God rewards a life of worship, sacrifice, and prayer done in secret for him.

Grow in Grace

Spend time in secret with God today. If possible, remove all distractions and go to a place where you can pray, read the Word, and fellowship with your Maker.

85

HE KNOWS YOUR NAME

Not to us, O LORD, not to us, but to your name give glory,
for the sake of your steadfast love and your faithfulness!

PSALM 115:1

Have you ever wondered about all the people in the Bible who are mentioned yet unnamed and often unnoticed? We know about Moses leading the Israelites out of Egypt, through the Red Sea, and into the wilderness, but what about the fathers who carried their children, walking on the sandy seabed with walls of water on either side? Or the women who gave birth in a temporary tent while wandering in the wilderness?

Then there's the Shunammite woman who cared for the prophet Elisha (see 2 Kings 4:8-37). We peer into her story and see her heart, her home, and her longing for a child, yet we don't know her name.

There's also the Samaritan woman who met Jesus at the well and was given the living water that always satisfies and never runs dry (see John 4:1-45). Though she is nameless to us, God knows her name.

The nameless God-fearing people mentioned in the Bible tell of God's love for hidden acts of faithfulness. He does not search for the greatest, most popular, or most successful people to adopt into his family. He looks beneath the surface, to the heart (see 1 Samuel 16:7). We are not called to be the main character in the story of redemption; we are simply called to be faithful in our supporting roles as God's children. Even when people we esteem don't know our names or notice our efforts, we are seen by God.

While the Israelites were in Babylonian exile due to their unrepentant idolatry, God spoke to them through the prophet Isaiah: "Thus says the LORD, he who created you, O Jacob, he who formed you, O Israel: 'Fear not, for I have redeemed you; *I have called you by name, you are mine*'" (Isaiah 43:1, emphasis added). God did not reject or forget his people; he called them by name and reminded them that they were his. They were not possessions of the Babylonians. They were not defined by their suffering, shame, or repeated failure. They were his, and he knew them by name.

God knows the nameless, and he knows those who feel named by their past sins and present struggles. He knows those who are not recorded on the pages of history, and he knows those who remain unseen for their whole lives. He knows the missionary serving and sharing the gospel in a remote location, and he knows the mother who spends her days shepherding the souls of her children. He notices the unnoticed, and he loves the ordinary.

His grace covers us, his redemption keeps us, and his calling sustains us. He has called us by name, and we are his forever.

Word before World
God knows your name, and you are his.

Grow in Grace
Think of a time when you felt unnoticed or unimportant.
What would it look like to relive that scene
with the knowledge that God named you and
acknowledged you in that moment?

86

FIVE MINUTES

Seek the LORD and his strength;
seek his presence continually!
1 CHRONICLES 16:11

Five minutes in the Word is better than no time in the Word. Five minutes in prayer is better than no time in prayer. When life is packed to the brim and every minute is accounted for, with something to do or someplace to be, time with God often gets squeezed out. We think if we can't fit in extended time in deep Bible study, why bother trying? In the scope of time, five minutes might not seem like much, but when stacked together, five-minute increments have an impact on the course of our days.

Five more minutes, we tell ourselves as we scroll on our phone, attempting to escape stress and chaos. Even though the buzz of online chatter doesn't satisfy us, it often seems easier to choose that noise over the unsettling quiet of our own souls.

Five more minutes, we rationalize as we press snooze again. Five more minutes of sleep inches towards thirty, and before we know it, we've run out of time to read our Bible—again.

What if we challenged our mindset on how we spend five-minute pockets of time? Instead of choosing to zone out, what if we chose to zoom our vision onto the Lord?

There are many days I begin reading my Bible, only to be interrupted within the first five minutes. I want to throw my hands in the air in frustration, but I've learned that God can speak even in just one verse. He can multiply the five minutes I have to offer into a fruitful time with him, just as he multiplied five loaves of bread and two fish to feed thousands of people (see Matthew 14:13-21; John 6:1-13). He is not limited by time, and his Word accomplishes what it sets out to do (see Isaiah 55:10-11). Scripture revives us and restores us—even in one verse, even if the thirty minutes you planned to read your Bible turned into five.

What if we changed our perspective on the little pockets of time scattered throughout our days? What if we spent the five minutes we sit in the drive-through or the carpool line meditating on a Scripture memory verse? Or what if we used the five-minute breaks between meetings to pray over what is worrying us and give thanks to God, who will sustain us for what we are going to do next? What if we opened our Bibles for just five minutes while standing at the stove waiting for water to boil for dinner? These pockets of time can become moments of rest and refreshment when we use them to focus on the Lord.

You don't have to spend hours in Bible study, prayer, or meditation to reap a harvest from God's Word. God is with you as you go through your day. Five minutes over the course of your days can turn into a lifetime of seeking God.

Word before World
God can multiply the time we spend with him,
even if it's just five minutes at a time.

Grow in Grace
Give God your five minutes, and then resolve to
dig in deeper and spend more time with him. Feast on
God's Word as you go about your day, and use the five-
minute pockets to bring your mind back to him.

87

THE BEST IS YET TO COME

I am sure of this, that he who began a good work
in you will bring it to completion at the day of Jesus Christ.

PHILIPPIANS 1:6

When my husband and I were newlyweds, we lived near the Smoky Mountains and hiked as often as we could. One hike in particular tried my faith in my husband's choice of trails. While he grew up exploring the great outdoors, I didn't start hiking until we got married. When I envisioned a hiking adventure, what came to mind was a short trip to a waterfall and back, not a strenuous eight-hour trek on a lonely trail. But he'd done this hike before, and he knew the result would be worth the many miles (and many complaints from me along the way).

"When are we going to see a pretty view?" I asked. "I'm so hungry. Are there bears out here? Is this going to be worth it? Where's the bathroom? I'm so tired. My legs feel like jelly." On and on I went, as we traversed the uphill trail, complaining to my ever-so-patient husband.

When we finally reached our destination, I took it all back—every complaint, every sigh, every doubt, every fear that we'd come across a bear and have to run for our lives. The panorama of endless hills blanketed by trees that looked like tiny specks of broccoli took my breath away. My husband knew the show-stopping view that awaited our arduous journey, and he meant it when he said, "The best is yet to come."

Sometimes our journey of sanctification and growing in Christ-likeness feels like an endless uphill hike. We forget God's past faithfulness and worry that his promises will fail. We despise the mundane routines that make up the bulk of our days and wonder what good God could produce in our hearts as we go to work, fix dinner, and fold laundry yet again.

In his letter to the church at Philippi, the apostle Paul assures believers of God's continual work of sanctification in their lives. He says, "I am sure of this, that he who began a good work in you will bring it to completion at the day of Jesus Christ" (Philippians 1:6). God will finish the work he has started in our hearts. Even when we are facing an arduous journey and we wonder when reprieve will come, he is still doing good, because he *is* good.

God is using the daily happenings in your life to scrub your soul and shape your desires to be more like his. He is giving you the endurance you need to keep putting one foot in front of the other. He is removing idols from the throne of your heart that can never satisfy. He is giving you opportunities to see his faithfulness on display (see 1 John 3:2).

God is always doing good in the lives of his people, even when we can't see the end result or understand his means. The best truly is yet to come for those who place their trust in him.

Word before World
God is still doing good in the midst of your
wandering, waiting, and wondering.

Grow in Grace
The next time you feel tempted to complain about your
circumstances, look for the good God is doing and
the ways he is shaping your heart to be like his.

88

DEPENDENT ON OUR DEPENDABLE GOD

He spread a cloud for a covering, and fire to give light by night.
They asked, and he brought quail, and gave them bread from heaven in abundance.
He opened the rock, and water gushed out; it flowed through the desert like
a river. For he remembered his holy promise, and Abraham, his servant.

PSALM 105:39-42

I slipped out the door of my daughter's room and leaned my head on the scuffed-up wall in front of me. *I'm such a failure,* I thought as I heard my baby crying and one of my sons yelling for me downstairs. *I'm failing as a mother, failing as a friend, failing at organizing our home and our schedule, failing at keeping my attitude like Christ's.*

The list could go on, but at the core is the belief that I have to be perfect. If perfection is the bar I'm reaching for, then I *am* failing. I am failing at being limitless. I am failing at being God. That's because I was never meant to be perfect or limitless, and I certainly wasn't meant to be God.

I am created; he is my Creator. I am bound by time, by the ticking of the clock, and by the restraints of my body; he is eternal, limitless, omnipresent. I am imperfect and dependent; he is perfect and perfectly dependable.

I slid to the floor as I listened to my baby wrestling herself to sleep in her crib. She was overtired, and so was I. She's dependent on me to care for her—to provide food and protection and even to put her down for a nap. *Dependent*. This three-syllable word swirls around in my head. What an accurate way to view who I am too.

I am dependent on my dependable God, I repeat to myself as I walk down the stairs. Life looks different through this filter. More hopeful. More faithful. More grateful. More joy-*full*.

During the Israelites' forty-year stint of wandering in the wilderness, they were utterly dependent on God. They depended on God for direction, so he led them with a pillar of cloud by day and a pillar of fire by night (see Exodus 13:21). They depended on God for victory, and he taught them countless times that victory belonged to him (see Exodus 14:18; 17:15-16). They depended on God for food, so he rained down a mysterious bread from heaven called manna (see Exodus 16:4). They depended on God for water, and God provided through a rock (see Exodus 17:1-7). They depended on God for wisdom about how to live, so God provided the Law (see Exodus 20-24). They depended on God for a place of worship, and God provided the Tabernacle (see Exodus 25-40).

But their dependence did not end once their wandering was over. Once they were in the Promised Land, they still depended on God for forgiveness and restoration. They still depended on God as they waited for the promised Messiah.

Why do we think we can live apart from the help of God? Our pride persuades us we can do everything on our own strength. We think we don't need to be forgiven because we haven't done anything *that* wrong, or we don't need God-fueled patience because we can muster it up from our own reserves, or we don't need help because we are self-sufficient. But the truth is, we are fully dependent on God—and he is fully dependable.

I pushed up from my kneeling position on the carpet and walked into my daughter's room, humbled by the Holy Spirit's conviction, hopeful in the help of my fully dependable God.

Word before World
We are dependent on our fully dependable God.

Grow in Grace
How have you labeled yourself a failure?
Does this line up with the truth of how God sees
you through the eyes of grace? How can you change your
perspective to focus on God's dependability to forgive,
provide, guide, and offer a fresh start in Jesus?

89

EVEN IF

Even if the fig tree does not blossom, and there is no fruit on the vines,
if the yield of the olive fails, and the fields produce no food, even if the flock
disappears from the fold, and there are no cattle in the stalls, yet I will triumph in
the LORD, I will rejoice in the God of my salvation. The Lord GOD is my strength,
and He has made my feet like deer's feet, and has me walk on my high places.

HABAKKUK 3:17-19, NASB

They are age-old questions: Why do the wicked flourish? Why does sin prevail? And why is our rescue delayed longer than we'd like? These questions surface frequently throughout Scripture. They're asked by ordinary people and prophets, kings and followers of God who abide by his law.

Habakkuk, an Old Testament prophet to the southern kingdom of Judah, began his oracle by asking God the same questions.

During this time in Israel's history, the Chaldeans (also referred to as the Babylonians) were rising to power. Habakkuk wrestled with their victories over God's people, and he questioned God: "Why do you idly look at wrong?" (Habakkuk 1:3).

Habakkuk did not mince words, nor did he turn away from God. He went to God with his complaints and questions, and God answered him and revealed his greater purpose: he was raising up the Chaldeans as a judgment for the Israelites' disobedience (see verses 5-12). Habakkuk seemed to have a moment of understanding and insight, but then he pressed further: "Why do you idly look at traitors and remain silent when the wicked swallows up the man more righteous than he?" (verse 13).

God responded with yet another reminder of his swiftness to offer mercy and his perfect timing to bring salvation. He reminded Habakkuk that his word never fails: "If it seems slow, wait for it; it will surely come; it will not delay" (Habakkuk 2:3). God widened Habakkuk's narrow vision and helped him see that the wicked don't get away with sin forever, but the righteous will live by faith (see verse 4).

Hope in God's mercy and justice hinges on our willingness to believe he will fulfill his promises. By faith we ask God "Why?" and by faith we receive reminders of his character. By faith, we wait, watch, and listen for God's plans to unfurl, and by faith, we repent of our sins, receive his forgiveness, and rejoice in his salvation (see Psalm 73).

Have you ever found yourself in Habakkuk's position, questioning why God allows the wicked to flourish? I know I have. I ask these questions when I read the news, when I hear about another injustice, or when I struggle to grasp why Christians around the world face relentless persecution for their faith in Jesus.

In the end, God turned Habakkuk's "Why?" questions into "Even if" statements of faith. Habakkuk saw a sliver of God's providence, and he decided to wait in faith (see Habakkuk 3:17-19).

He resolved to trust in God and rejoiced in him . . . *even if* the very worst happened. It is by faith that we believe God is good, God is just, and God is faithful, even when our physical eyes can't see it.

Word before World

We can ask God "Why?" when life doesn't make sense.
And we can hold on to hope, even if our circumstances look
bleak from a human perspective. God is still at work.

Grow in Grace

When was the last time you asked God "Why?"
Write out your own "Even if" statements, committing
to put your hope in God no matter what comes.

90

FAITH ON THE FRINGES

When the woman saw that she was not hidden, she came trembling,
and falling down before him declared in the presence of all the people
why she had touched him, and how she had been immediately healed.

LUKE 8:47

The conversation was going places where I wasn't invited. My friends started a discussion that didn't include me, and all of a sudden I felt lonely even though I was surrounded by a crowd of women who knew me.

Have you ever felt the pangs of being left out—unseen by family, friends, or colleagues? In these moments, we have a choice: we can either retreat inward or reach outward for help, healing, and wholeness in Christ. In this fallen world, we frequently encounter situations that leave us feeling isolated and alone. It's possible to be in a crowd and still feel unseen and overlooked.

As we see in the Gospels, Jesus didn't ignore, leave out, or pass by those on the fringes; he paused, looked them in the eyes, and spoke to them. One particular encounter of Jesus' compassion for the lonely and overlooked moves me every time I read it.

Luke 8 recounts a time when Jesus was surrounded by a large crowd of people who were waiting for him. Luke describes the rambunctious crowd as pressing all around Jesus. He was being touched and called out to from all sides.

In the midst of the crowd was a woman who had been bleeding for twelve straight years. *Twelve years*—that's 4,380 days (give or take). Not only was this woman a social outcast due to her infirmity, but she was also broke. She'd spent all her money searching for a cure, but no one could heal her.

She came behind Jesus, reached out, and touched the edge of his clothing. Immediately her bleeding ceased (see Luke 8:44).

Jesus stopped and asked, "Who was it that touched me?" (Luke 8:45).

Peter, one of the disciples, reminded Jesus that he was being touched by a whole multitude of people. Jesus clarified, "Someone has touched me, for I perceive that power has gone out from me" (Luke 8:46).

Can you imagine what the crowd was thinking? They must have thought Jesus was confused. And yet only *one* person had touched the fringes of his garment with faith in his salvation.

When Jesus called out to the crowd, asking who had touched him, this woman "saw she was not hidden" and came before him, trembling. Jesus looked at her—a woman who was left out, alone, impoverished, and untouchable—and said, "Daughter, your faith has made you well; go in peace" (Luke 8:47-48).

Her recorded moment with Jesus ends here, and yet her faith in her Savior lives on.

We serve a Savior who sees those who are on the fringes—those who are left out, lonely, insecure, and alone (see Psalm 34:5). When he healed the bleeding woman, her ultimate salvation was not in the physical relief from her infirmity but in the healing of her sin-stained soul.

Because of Jesus' great love and power, we go forward in peace, confident in our identity in him. Instead of turning inward in defeat, we can turn outward and look to him for hope, encouragement, and comfort—even when we feel unseen in a crowd.

Word before World
In Christ, you are seen, known, and loved.

Grow in Grace
When you feel left out, instead of retreating inward in defeat,
insecurity, or discouragement, look upward to Christ.

91

A BROKEN MEASURING STICK

Not that we dare to classify or compare ourselves with some of those who are
commending themselves. But when they measure themselves by one another
and compare themselves with one another, they are without understanding.

2 CORINTHIANS 10:12

We carry it like a cane, leaning our weight on it. It bruises our sides, cuts our hands, and causes us to trip. We pack it in our purses and our suitcases, squeeze it into diaper bags and backpacks, and make sure we have it when we go out with friends.

What is this possession we hold so dear and cling so tightly to? It's the measuring stick of comparison.

Whether we use it as a crutch, a weapon, or a scepter to rule our little kingdoms, the measuring stick of comparison is the most cumbersome accessory we can carry. It chains us to the past, keeps us trapped in discontentment, and leaves us wounded and wanting.

We pull it out to measure ourselves against our neighbor. We use it to justify our actions, judge our friends and acquaintances, and exalt our ego. At the same time, it strips us of peace, makes us stumble in discouragement, and sucks us into a spiral of despondency.

The measuring stick of comparison is not a support to our wounded souls; it's a hindrance to loving God wholeheartedly and loving our neighbor as ourselves.

Comparison is an age-old trap of the enemy to distract us from a life of faithfulness to God. Satan offers it to us in moments of weakness and weariness. Instead of grasping our Savior's hand for help, we take hold of our measuring stick and start comparing our lives to someone else's.

When we use it, we either think too highly of ourselves or berate ourselves. When we see someone who is gifted in a way we're not, we get down on ourselves, doubting that God could ever use us. *How can I measure up to her? What do I have to offer?* When we encounter someone who isn't gifted the way we are, we become puffed up, thinking we are God's answer to the world's problems. *What would they do without me? I could do that better than they could.*

Comparison steals our joy in life, disrupts our unity with other believers, and lessens our love for one another. Beneath the surface of comparison is envy. We want to be like our neighbor and have what our neighbor has while forgetting God's purposes for us (see 1 Corinthians 13:4; Galatians 5:26). We think, *If only I were like her, my life would be better.* We want what we do not have, and we do not want what we *do* have (see James 4:2-3).

So what do we do with these measuring sticks we carry? Instead of looking around us, we turn our gaze to our Savior, who hung on two beams of wood nailed together to form a cross (see 1 Peter 2:24). When we come to Christ, who was broken for our sin, he takes our measuring sticks and breaks them in two.

In his hands of grace, he fashions together the pieces of our measuring stick and transforms them into a new shape for us to carry: the shape of a cross (see Luke 9:23).

Word before World
The cure for comparison is to gaze steadily on the cross of Christ.

Grow in Grace
When are you most tempted to pull out your comparison measuring stick? What would it look like to lay that stick down the next time you see someone you envy (see Ephesians 4:12-16)?

92

HOLY SPIRIT, HERE'S MY PLANNER

The heart of man plans his way,
but the LORD establishes his steps.

PROVERBS 16:9

Every day we make plans and fill our agendas with meetings, projects, and tasks that need to get done. But rarely does a day go as planned. Your child spills milk on your shirt right before you walk out the door. You get ready to leave, only to realize your work pants are still at the dry cleaner. You are running behind, only to be rear-ended by the car behind you. You get sidetracked and forget to make that important call. You plan a trip to the beach, only to be forced to cancel at the last minute because a hurricane hits the exact spot you were planning to go.

The days that have gone exactly as I planned are so rare that I can't recall a single one off the top of my head. There's always something that doesn't go the way I anticipate—something that causes me to pivot, reevaluate, and redirect. When this happens, my first response is often to count my losses, naming all the things that are going wrong instead of asking God for eyes to see how he's at work. If you, too, find yourself struggling to let go of your plans, pull up a chair with me and let's learn from the wisdom of James:

Come now, you who say, "Today or tomorrow we will go into such and such a town and spend a year there and trade and make a profit"—yet you do not know what tomorrow will bring. What is your life? For you are a mist that appears for a little time and then vanishes. Instead you ought to say, "If the Lord wills, we will live and do this or that."
JAMES 4:13-15

James revealed three important truths to keep in mind as we plan our days:

1. **Our lives are temporary.** James describes our lives as a mist, as steam that rises and then—*poof!*—vanishes as quickly as it appeared. This is a humbling reality check. Living with the knowledge that our lives are just a vapor helps us see our plans from an eternal perspective.

2. **We do not know what tomorrow will bring.** Our understanding is limited, finite; God's understanding is unlimited, infinite. We don't know what tomorrow will bring, but we know the God who holds tomorrow. With this comforting knowledge in mind, we can live faithfully in this moment, trusting God to provide for our needs.

3. **God's plans, not ours, come to pass.** Making plans is not wrong, but building our lives on them leads to a shaky foundation. James encourages us to make plans with this caveat: "If the Lord wills." We bring our plans into alignment with his by being in the Word, in prayer, and in fellowship with other believers.

What if we gave the Holy Spirit our planners each day and welcomed him into the creation of our schedules as well as the changes?

Today, I invite you to pray along with me: "Holy Spirit, here is my planner. Here is my life, my dreams, my goals, my pursuits, my loves, my family, my passions, my joys, and my days." In this act of surrender and handing over the pen comes a freedom and peace that's even better than having your day unfold exactly the way you planned.

Word before World

Plan your days remembering that
your life is a vapor and
eternity with Christ is forever.
Live for what will last.

Grow in Grace

As you jot down tasks in your planner
or add them to your calendar,
ask the Holy Spirit to guide you.
Surrender your plans
to the sovereign will of God.

UNDONE

If we live by the Spirit,
let us also keep in step with the Spirit.

GALATIANS 5:25

O Lord, I have so much to do
But not the energy to do it all.
My appetite for productivity
Is greater than my appetite for you.

I treasure
Moving forward,
Making progress,
Having something to show
For the hours I lived.

I desire
To be known,
To be seen,
To be thanked,
To be affirmed.

My flesh rages
Against communion with you.
My mind wrestles

To be at peace.
My fingers tighten
Rather than let go.

I admit—
Being still
Is harder
Than being productive.

Being quiet
Is harder
Than speaking up.

Being prayerful
Is harder
Than making plans.

Forgive me
For loving my lists
More than I love you.
I confess
My short-sighted desires,
And I request
An eternal-minded heart.

There will always be more to do
And not enough energy to get it done.
Help me to choose you
And learn how to leave loose ends
Undone.[1]

Word before World

You only have a limited amount of time and
energy each day. Ask the Lord to show you
what his priorities are, and learn to leave
what cannot be completed, undone.

Grow in Grace

Do you take pride in placing a checkmark
next to the items on your task list?
Confess your desire to be able to
do all things in your own strength, and
surrender your time and energy to the Lord.

94

SHE GAVE HER ALL;
HE GAVE HER MORE

Fear not, for I am with you; be not dismayed,
for I am your God; I will strengthen you, I will help you,
I will uphold you with my righteous right hand.

ISAIAH 41:10

When my faith starts to fizzle, I spark it back to life with the faith of others. One way I do this is by reading Christian biographies. One biography that was especially formative for my faith was about Gladys Aylward and her missionary journey to China. Her story is marked by persecution and physical suffering, but woven throughout it is the thread of God's goodness and the power of the gospel.

Burdened for those who had not heard the gospel, Gladys left the comfort of her home and family in her late twenties and headed to China. Her journey was full of unexpected challenges. At one point she became stuck in Russia, unable to travel to her final destination. As she shivered in the frigid weather, afraid she would freeze to death, she asked the Lord, "O God, is it worth it?"[1]

How many times have we asked the same thing? Is this our response when trials surround us and squeeze out our hope? When each step of obedience we take is met with a new hurdle?

When we cry out to God, like Gladys, and ask, "O God, is it worth it?" he answers with the cross. If the Son of God suffered to save us and set us free, then we will know him more intimately through suffering (see Romans 8:32; Philippians 3:8-12). This was true for Gladys, and it's true for us.

Gladys Aylward gave her life for the cause of Christ. She surrendered every earthly comfort to show that Jesus is our only eternal hope. She went without food, loved those in prison, cared for orphans, and shared about Jesus with her actions and words with every person she came into contact with.

During her tenure in Yangcheng, she helped set up and run an inn and eventually helped deliver one hundred orphans out of China during the War of Resistance against Japanese Aggression. Her faith was not always strong, but God's strength held her through her moments of weakness.

After her prayer, Gladys was comforted by these words: "Be not afraid, remember I am the Lord."

The riches of gaining Christ far exceed anything we might lose in this life. As Paul said, everything is loss (literally, "rubbish"[2]) compared to knowing Christ (see Philippians 3:7-9). When we stand before the throne of God, we will see with unhindered vision how everything in this world is rubbish compared to the glory of knowing Jesus.

So go forward in faith as you share the gospel and follow God's leading. As you do, remember these comforting words God gave Gladys in Russia: "Be not afraid, remember I am the Lord."

Word before World

Everything you could lose for following Jesus is worth
everything you will gain in knowing him.

Grow in Grace

What circumstances in your life have caused you to ask,
"O God, is it worth it?" When doubts creep in,
remember the sacrifices Jesus made on your behalf,
and trust that he will redeem any trials you face.

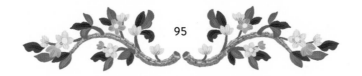

95

HIDDEN FAITHFULNESS

Whatever you do, work at it with all your heart, as working for the Lord,
not for human masters, since you know that you will receive an inheritance
from the Lord as a reward. It is the Lord Christ you are serving.

COLOSSIANS 3:23-24. NIV

id you notice I vacuumed the living room?"

We'd just sat down for dinner when this question popped out of my mouth. It had been a long day of doing work that felt unimportant. No one applauded me for scrubbing stained toilets or gave me a pat on the back when I unloaded the dishwasher. No one cheered me on as I paid bills or completed my work. No one gave me a high five when I finished vacuuming the living room. I was desperate for words of affirmation, longing to be seen and noticed for my hard work. I wanted to know that my behind-the-scenes faithfulness was worth it in the grand scheme of things.

The majority of our lives is spent doing ordinary, unseen tasks. Shiny, center stage moments don't usually challenge our character or refine our motives; it's the backstage activity no one sees that forms and transforms us. The thankless tasks we do—necessary, unexciting things like collecting the garbage, wiping runny noses, or balancing a spreadsheet—reveal what our hearts truly treasure. Do we crave the praise of others? Or do we value these hidden tasks as opportunities to quietly serve our faithful God?

After God gave the Israelites detailed instructions about the building and assembly of the Tabernacle, Moses asked the people of Israel, specifically those with generous hearts, to give the materials and labor needed (see Exodus 35:5).

The response was stunning: "They came, everyone whose heart stirred him, and everyone whose spirit moved him, and brought the LORD's contribution to be used for the tent of meeting, and for all its service, and for the holy garments" (Exodus 35:21). Skilled women spun yarns, linen, and goats' hair (see verses 25-26). Leaders brought their prized treasures for the priest's ephod, along with spices and oil for lamps and offerings (see verses 27-28). Anyone whose "heart moved them" brought what they had and gave it to the Lord.

What if instead of giving freely of their possessions, time, and skills, they had demanded that a plaque be bolted outside the Tabernacle applauding them for their sacrifice? What if the women who had spent countless hours spinning yarn required that they be praised for their time and talent?

The Tabernacle was built not by people seeking fame but by ordinary people with extraordinary love for God. The apostle Paul writes, "*Whatever you do*, work at it with *all your heart*, as working for the Lord, not for human masters, since you know that you will receive an inheritance from the Lord as a reward. It is the Lord Christ you are serving" (Colossians 3:23-24, emphasis added). Paul doesn't say, "Whenever you do something special and exciting that everyone praises you for, work at it with all your heart. But you can do the unfancy, boring stuff no one sees with half the effort." Paul brings us back to the heart of faithfulness, serving, and generosity. We do it for the Lord, not for the praise of man.

When Christ is our treasure and our hearts are stirred by the Holy Spirit, any task set before us is worth our wholehearted effort—for the glory of God and for the honor of his name. Even vacuuming up Cheerios.

Word before World

Everything we do is seen by God—
including the backstage, boring activities.
Whatever you are doing,
do it for the glory of his name.

Grow in Grace

Meditate on Psalm 100:2,
which tells us to serve the Lord with gladness.
What would it look like to do thankless tasks
with gladness and love for God today?

96

THE UNSEARCHABLE THINGS OF GOD

Call to me and I will answer you and tell you great
and unsearchable things you do not know.

JEREMIAH 33:3, NIV

In the past when I read devotionals by theologians, pastors, and heroes of the faith, I would ache to experience the same intimacy with God I sensed in them. *Can I read the Bible with the same confidence and understanding?* I wondered. *Or do some people have a direct line to Jesus reserved for elite Christians?*

In the book of Jeremiah, the prophet was sent by God to foretell impending judgment on the Israelites for their idolatry. Not only would they be exiled from the Promised Land, but they would also be taken captive by the ruthless Babylonians. Cushioned within Jeremiah's messages were unbreakable threads of hope for the people to cling to in the midst of judgment and exile.

Jeremiah 31:33 says, "This is the covenant that I will make with the house of Israel after those days, declares the LORD: I will put my law within them, and I will write it on their hearts. And I will be their God, and they shall be my people." Resolute in their waywardness, the Israelites rejected Jeremiah and threw him in prison. While he was in chains, Jeremiah heard the word of the Lord again: "Call to me and I will answer you and tell you great and unsearchable things you do not know" (Jeremiah 33:3).

God's invitation for his people to come to him was given to them not because they had their act together but because of his mercy and love. The Israelites were not perfect, yet God called them, showering his grace on their heads. We must remember this when we begin to think that only "perfect" Christians can call out to God and mine treasures from the depths of his Word.

Romans 3:23 explains, "All have sinned and fall short of the glory of God." There are no perfect Christians, only redeemed Christians. There is no exclusive hotline to get God's attention—we have all been given access to the throne of grace through the sacrifice of Jesus Christ.

The people we read about, look up to, and learn from all struggle like we do. They wrestle like we do. They doubt like we do. But they press on and press in further. They repent of their sin and turn to God. They call out to him, confident that he will answer.

The same invitation that God gave the Israelites in Jeremiah 33:3 is given to us in Christ: "In him, you also, when you heard the word of truth, the gospel of your salvation, and believed in him, were sealed with the promised Holy Spirit, who is the guarantee of our inheritance until we acquire possession of it, to the praise of his glory" (Ephesians 1:13-14).

In Christ, you have been given full access to the throne of God, and the Holy Spirit now dwells in you (see 1 Corinthians 6:19). When you're tempted to look to a pastor or a Bible teacher and place them on a pedestal, or when you find yourself relying on their words above the Word of God, remember that they are human, just like us.

So open your Bible, seek the Lord with all your heart, and delight in the unsearchable things he delights to show you.

Word before World
The same God who spoke through Jeremiah is the same God who speaks to us through Christ and invites us into the mysteries of the gospel.

Grow in Grace
Do you long to hear from God the way your pastor, Bible study leader, or favorite theologian does? You can! Be willing to linger in God's presence as you ask him to teach through his Word.

97

EMBRACING INTERRUPTIONS

Rising very early in the morning, while it was still dark,
he departed and went out to a desolate place, and there he prayed.

MARK 1:35

Some days feel like a continuous string of interruptions. From the moment my feet hit the floor in the morning, I ping-pong from diaper changes to unexpected deadlines to snack cleanup to requests that upend my entire agenda for the day.

On days like this, when productivity feels impossible and interruptions multiply, I remind myself of how Jesus handled distractions. He didn't turn little children away; he welcomed them onto his lap (see Mark 10:13-16). He didn't scold the bleeding woman who touched the hem of his garment while he was on his way to Jairus's home. Instead, he healed her (see Luke 8:40-48). Jesus was the ultimate example of how to handle interruptions with grace and purpose.

In Mark's Gospel, we see a glimpse into Jesus' relationship with the Father while he was on earth. "Rising very early in the morning, while it was still dark, he departed and went out to a desolate place, and there he prayed" (Mark 1:35). Though we aren't given many details in this short verse, we know Jesus intentionally woke up early and went to a solitary place to spend time with his Father and pray. The quiet never lasted, though, because right after this, Jesus faced the same thing you and I face: interruptions. "Simon and those who were with him searched for him, and they found him and said to him, 'Everyone is looking for you'" (verses 36-37).

Jesus understands how it feels to be interrupted when spending time alone in prayer. Jesus didn't rebuke Simon for interrupting his solitude. He didn't snap at his disciples or complain about how they interrupted his quiet time. He said to them, "Let us go on to the next towns, that I may preach there also, for that is why I came out" (verse 38). Jesus responded with patience, grace, and purpose. He tended to their needs and reminded them of his mission—and theirs.

This morning I woke up before anyone else in the house with the intention of reading God's Word. After pouring my coffee, I grabbed my Bible from the end table and sat down on our well-worn couch. Like clockwork, I heard a *thump* upstairs, a door open, and a little voice at the top of the stairs whispering, "I want to come snuggle downstairs."

My children have a sixth sense for when I need alone time or time with God. In those moments when everything within me wants to turn them away, I'm reminded of the grace of Jesus. Sometimes I do tell them to play in their room while I spend time in God's Word, and sometimes I invite them to sit and read with me. I don't always respond with grace, but God always extends his grace anyway.

Perhaps the distractions we face when reading God's Word are his whispers to us to slow down and remember that we need him. Maybe the child who calls for us when we are working or the friend who asks to chat when we are heading somewhere is his ministry for us today.

When seen through the eyes of Christ, interruptions aren't delays or intrusions at all; they are opportunities to live out the Word and follow the footsteps of our King.

Word before World

Interruptions are inevitable, but by God's grace,
we can see them as opportunities to live like Christ,
love others, and trust God with each moment.

Grow in Grace

How do you typically respond if you're interrupted
when you are reading the Word? Ask the Lord to
cultivate a spirit of patience and joy in you so
you can respond in a way that honors him.

WHAT DAY IS TODAY?

This is the day that the LORD has made;
let us rejoice and be glad in it.

PSALM 118:24

I often start the day by asking my kids, "What day is today?"

By now they know how to respond, "The day the Lord has made!"

"And what are we to do?" I ask.

"Rejoice and be glad in it!"

Before you begin to think this moment is always special, just yesterday I asked the boys this question, and my youngest son responded in a huff, "Why do you ask us that *every single day*?"

The answer lies in the question, because every day we face new challenges that shroud our memory and lure us to forget God's faithfulness. We need to shake our souls awake with the reminder that God has made this day, and because he is in control, we can rejoice and be glad in the minutes we've been given.

It's easy to reserve rejoicing in the Lord for days that flow seamlessly and are laced with magical moments. But God has also made the days when we experience heartache, discouragement, and suffering. In seasons when I battled anxiety and when hope felt like a distant dream, I dug deeper into the meaning of Psalm 118:24. How could

I rejoice and be glad when everything within me was shouting the exact opposite?

The verses leading up to Psalm 118:24 provide context for this passage. The psalmist says, "I thank you that you have answered me and have become my salvation. The stone that the builders rejected has become the cornerstone. This is the LORD's doing; it is marvelous in our eyes" (verses 21-23). David, who was likely the writer of Psalm 118, had been like a rejected stone, yet God chose him to be the king of Israel.[1]

The ultimate fulfillment of this psalm came through Jesus Christ. Jesus referenced this passage multiple times, and several other New Testament writers mentioned it as well (see Matthew 21:42; Mark 12:10-11; Acts 4:11; and 1 Peter 2:7-8).

When Jesus quoted this psalm, he was on his way to Jerusalem, where he would be crucified. As he entered Jerusalem on a donkey, people in the crowd spread their cloaks onto the dirt for him, saying, "Hosanna to the Son of David! Blessed is he who comes in the name of the Lord! Hosanna in the highest!" (Matthew 21:9) When Jesus entered Jerusalem, he came as King—the chief cornerstone who would later be rejected by the same people who were now celebrating him.

Because Christ is King over everything, exalted now and forever, we can rejoice and be glad in *this day*. Salvation, redemption, and hope are found in Jesus, who lived the life we could not live, died the death we deserved to die, and was raised to life so we could have eternal life in him.

When your heart is filled with anxiety or despair, remember Christ, who suffered and bought your salvation. Then ask yourself, *What day is today?* Because you live in the shadow of the cross of Christ and the light of his redemption, you can answer with confidence, "This is the day the Lord has made. I will rejoice and be glad in it!"

Word before World

Because Christ is King over everything,
we can rejoice and be glad in his faithfulness today.

Grow in Grace

Write Psalm 118:24 on a notecard
and place it somewhere you'll see it
often as a reminder that today is the day the
Lord has made. He will bring you through.

99

SANDCASTLE KINGDOMS

*Everyone then who hears these words of mine and does them
will be like a wise man who built his house on the rock.*

MATTHEW 7:24

I'll admit, there are many days I build a sandcastle kingdom with my time and energy. I pack my bags and head into the world to begin my construction. Perhaps you've gathered with me at the water's edge, where the hopes and dreams of our hearts meet the day-to-day routines of our lives. We lug our buckets filled with pride and our shovels of self-sufficiency to the shoreline and dig, shape, and mold our sandcastle kingdoms. When we notice the waves inching closer to our precious creations, we try to protect them, but in the end, they wash away. The next day, we start all over again.

Jesus invites us to build on the foundation of a better Kingdom—one that no waves, worries, or windstorms can destroy, a Kingdom built on the Rock. Jesus illustrated this by comparing two builders: the wise builder and the foolish builder (see Matthew 7:24-27). The wise person builds their house (meaning their life) on the rock. The foolish person builds their life on what is temporary, the sand.

Jesus explained that the wise builder is like the person who hears the Word of God and acts on it. The foolish builder, however, is like the person who listens to the words of Jesus and turns away from him. The wise person takes into account future storms and torrential rains that will come and digs a deep foundation, past the hardened summer sand and into the firm bedrock. The foolish person, in contrast, thinks only of the present moment and builds hastily on the sand, without taking into account future storms.

As native Galileans, the disciples would have understood the importance of building a house on a rocky foundation. The sand by the Sea of Galilee would harden during the summer, giving the appearance of a good foundation. But once the storms of winter came and the waters from the Jordan River rose, houses that had been built on the sand would collapse. Jesus used this real-life example to teach his followers how to build a life that matters eternally.

The truth is, every day we are building *something*. If we are not careful, we will be like the foolish builder and create our own sandcastle kingdoms. Jesus teaches us to build our lives on himself, the Rock (see 1 Peter 2:4-7), and he equips us with wisdom from the Word to do so.

Building your life on the Rock requires more work, more soul scrubbing, and more sacrifice than building on the sand. But in the end, building on him leads to abundant life—both here on earth and in eternity.

So loosen your grip on your sand-building tools, lay hold of eternal joy, and build your life on the Kingdom of God, which can never be shaken (see Hebrews 12:28).

Word before World

But Jesus rescues us from our flimsy sandcastle
kingdoms and invites us to be a part of building his
unshakable Kingdom (see Hebrews 12:28-29).

Grow in Grace

Ask the master builder, Jesus Christ,
to show you how to build your life on the Rock.

100

FAITHFUL ON EVERY PAGE

*God is faithful, by whom you were called into
the fellowship of his Son, Jesus Christ our Lord.*

1 CORINTHIANS 1:9

There has never been a single moment in all of history where God has not been faithful. You may be thinking, *But what about the times in my life when I can't see God's hand at work? Where is God in my suffering and sorrow? What about the prayers he doesn't seem to be answering?*

I've wrestled with these questions too, trying to understand the connection between what I *think* life should look like and the disheveled reality before me. It's easy for us to focus on the problems and questions we are unable to resolve instead of on God himself. When this happens, a fog of doubt descends on our perspective, making it almost impossible to see God at work.

But when we open the pages of Scripture, we see his faithfulness written on every page. All sixty-six books of the Bible make up one big story showcasing God's faithfulness. As we pore over the life-giving Word of God, the Holy Spirit blows the fog of doubt away, enabling us to see his providence in every story, every verse (see Luke 24:27; John 16:13).

In the books of the Law, God's faithfulness is displayed as he created the world and called it good (see Genesis 1:1-31) and in his promise to send a Savior to redeem his people (see Genesis 3:15) and make his people into a mighty nation (see Genesis 12:1-3). When the Israelites were in slavery in Egypt, his mighty hand delivered them out of bondage into freedom (see Exodus 2:24-25). After the building of the Tabernacle, God faithfully provided the sacrificial system to cleanse people from their sins and ultimately point them to Jesus (see Leviticus 1–10).

In the historical narratives, God faithfully led his people to the Promised Land and gave them victory over their enemies (see Joshua 1–5; 11:8-18). When the people asked for a king, God continued to be gracious, anointing a shepherd boy to rule over them. It was through King David's offspring that the promised Savior would one day be born (see 2 Samuel 7:16; Matthew 1:1).

In the Wisdom books, God faithfully supplied his people with words to pray, songs to sing, timeless wisdom to live by, and hope to hold on to in the midst of suffering (see Psalm 96; Proverbs 9:10; Psalm 42:11).

In the Prophets, God did not allow the idolatry of his people and the ruin of their souls to go unchecked. Rather, he faithfully sent messengers to declare his Word and to call his people to repent and to worship him alone (see Isaiah 30:15; Hosea 14:1-2). The prophets reminded people of God's faithfulness to provide justice for the oppressed and announced the coming of the Savior (see Isaiah 1:17; Micah 5:1-4).

In the Gospels, God sent his Son, Jesus Christ, as the promised Messiah (see Matthew 1). He lived the life we could not live, died the death we deserved to die, and was raised to life so we can have salvation by grace through faith (see Matthew 27–28).

In the Epistles, God worked in the church, the body of Christ, and faithfully changed his people into his likeness day by day (see 1 Corinthians 12:12-31; 2 Corinthians 3:18). God promises to finish the work he began in us and gives us guidance about how to treasure and proclaim the gospel of Jesus Christ (see Philippians 1:6-7).

In Revelation, God promised strength to endure persecution as we wait for Jesus to come again (see Revelation 2:10-11). His Word provides us with glimpses of the hope of our eternal home, where we will dwell with him forever (see Revelation 14:12; 21–22).

You are not exempt from the faithfulness of God, sister. Soak your soul in every verse of Scripture. Remember his tried-and-true promises (see 2 Corinthians 1:20). See his faithfulness to generations past, and build your life on the firm foundation of the gospel. Just as God was faithful to the patriarchs, the prophets, the Israelites fleeing Egypt, the disciples, and the early church, he will be faithful to you. The God who was, who is, and who is to come is always faithful—even in your life, even now.

Word before World

God's faithfulness is woven throughout
every page of Scripture, and
it is woven throughout your life story too.

Grow in Grace

When are you most prone to doubt God's faithfulness?
The next time you find yourself doubting his character,
pay attention to his activity in the pages of Scripture.
Praise him for being faithful to his people,
even when we are faithless (see 2 Timothy 2:13).

ACKNOWLEDGMENTS

When I was in the process of writing my first book, *The Well-Watered Woman*, an author friend told me, "A book is only as good as its editor." This saying has proved to be 100 percent true. Stephanie Rische, you are not only a five-star editor, you are a faithful steward of God's Word. Thank you for tightening my feeble words and adding clarity so God's Word is magnified.

To Kara Leonino: you're the engine behind this project, bringing my ideas to life and encouraging me in the moments when doubt tries to swallow my confidence in Christ. Thank you for cheering me on and caring for my heart every step of the way.

To Libby Dykstra and Dean Renninger: you are a dream design team! Your creativity and vision are woven into every page of this book. Thank you for helping me make a beautiful devotional!

To Laura Wifler and Ashlee Gadd: your conversations, pep talks, and dreams are dynamite to my creativity, writing, and passion to reach women with the hope of the gospel. Thank you for listening to me and loving me in the highs and the lows.

To Maggie Combs: your writing wisdom and prayers spurred me on as I wrote *Word before World*. You challenge me as a writer, a Christ follower, and a friend. Thank you for leading by example.

To Andrew Wolgemuth: thank you for faithfully sharing your wisdom and timely words of encouragement as I worked on this project. It is a gift to work alongside you!

To the Well-Watered Women team (Whitney Saville, Amelia Granberg, Erin Clack, Rachael Milner, Lauren Weir, Macie Mosely, Abbey Wysocki, Taylor Cage, Kercia Mueller, Andrea Jenkins, and Sarah Valentour): God has used each one of you to show me his love in a multitude of ways. Thank you for always pointing me to the goodness and faithfulness of Jesus.

To my husband, Greg: you are the unsung hero of every writing project I pursue. You serve our family with humility and joy, encourage me with God's Word, and love me in the heights and in the depths. Thank you, my love, for championing this message and doing whatever it takes to help it come to life!

To my parents, Ron and Kathy Jones: thank you for modeling what it looks like to faithfully put God's Word before the world. God has been weaving this message into my heart ever since I was a little girl. I'd wake up and find you poring over God's Word with a steaming cup of coffee in hand. Thank you for teaching me God's Word is life!

Nolan, Haddon, and Emelyn: you three delight your mama's heart to no end! There are many mornings I wake up to spend time in the Word only to have one of you crawling in my lap soon after. I pray you grow up to delight in God's Word—every moment of every day.

To my neighborhood Bible study friends: thank you for faithfully encouraging me to love God's Word. Our meetings in the park with our kids running wild have forever changed my heart. I am so grateful for your friendship!

Most importantly, to God, my Maker, Savior, and Friend: words fall short of the gratitude due to your name. This book would not exist apart from your grace, mercy, and steadfast love stirring my heart to the point I can do nothing else but write about your goodness! I have only begun to mine the depths and eternal truths you've revealed in your Word. I echo the psalmist's prayer in Psalm 119:18: "Open my eyes, that I may behold wondrous things out of your law." May my tiny hallelujahs add up to a mountain of praise that reaches to glory.

NOTES

DAY 3: PRESSED, BUT NOT CRUSHED

1. "Strong's #2346— thlíbō," Old and New Testament Greek Lexical Dictionary, StudyLight.org, https://www.studylight.org/lexicons/eng/greek/2346.html.

DAY 7: READ, WORSHIP, REPEAT

1. G. K. Chesterton, *Orthodoxy* (Chicago: Moody Publishers, 2009), 91–92.

DAY 24: TEARS OF MERCY

1. Douglas Main, "A Far Cry from Normal: Amazonian Butterflies Drink Turtle Tears," NBC News, September 12, 2013, https://www.nbcnews.com/science main/far-cry-normal-amazonian-butterflies-drink-turtle-tears-8c11138121; "Butterflies That Drink Turtle Tears for the Salt Content," The Kids Should See This, accessed October 20, 2023, https://thekidshouldseethis.com/post/turtle -tears-butterflies

2. "Crying Turtles: Deciphering Fact From Fiction," Smore Science, June 19, 2023, https://www.smorescience.com/do-turtles-cry/#:~:text=Land%20turtles %20or%20tortoises%20may,protecting%20them%20from%20potential %20harm.

DAY 31: GRIN AND LET GOD BEAR IT

1. "Strong's #6006—"âmaç," Old Testament Hebrew Lexical Dictionary, StudyLight .org,https://www.studylight.org/lexicons/eng/hebrew/6006.html.

DAY 33: WONDERSTRUCK

1. "'Cosmic Cliffs' in the Carina Nebula (NIRCam Image)," Webb Space Telescope, July 12, 2022, https://webbtelescope.org/contents/media/images/2022/031 /01G77PKB8NKR7S8Z6HBXMYATGJ.

DAY 36: SIMMER IN SCRIPTURE

1. "Strongs #1897—hâgâh," Old Testament Hebrew Lexical Dictionary, StudyLight .org, https://www.studylight.org/lexicons/eng/hebrew/1897.html.

DAY 47: THE PERFECT DAY

1. Randy Alcorn, *Heaven* (Carol Stream, IL: Tyndale House Publishers, 2004), 345.

DAY 54: EVERY HOUR I NEED THEE

1. C. Michael Hawn, "History of Hymns: 'I Need Thee Every Hour,'" Discipleship Ministries, The United Methodist Church, June 25, 2013, https://www.umc discipleship.org/resources/history-of-hymns-i-need-thee-every-hour.

DAY 56: SWEETER THAN HONEY

1. Patricia Polacco, *The Bee Tree* (New York: Puffin Books, 1998).

DAY 63: CATCHING FIREFLIES

1. "Synchronous Fireflies," Great Smoky Mountains, National Park Service, https://www.nps.gov/grsm/learn/nature/fireflies.htm.

DAY 68: BUT GOD . . .

1. Timothy Keller, *The Meaning of Marriage: Facing the Complexities of Commitment with the Wisdom of God* (New York: Penguin Books, 2013), 44.

DAY 71: EVEN WHEN YOU DON'T FEEL LIKE IT

1. C. S. Lewis, *The Weight of* Glory (New York: HarperCollins, 2001), 26.

DAY 75: TUNE YOUR HEART

1. Robert Robinson, "Come, Thou Fount of Every Blessing," hymnal.net, https:// www.hymnal.net/en/hymn/h/319.

DAY 77: THE SECRET IS THIS

1. Elisabeth Elliot, *Keep a Quiet Heart* (Ada, MI: Revell, 2012), 20.

DAY 78: BREATHE OUT WORRY

1. "Martin Luther," Biography.com, September 20, 2019, https://www.biography.com /religious-figures/martin-luther.

DAY 79: NOTHING LESS

1. Edward Mote, "My Hope Is Built on Nothing Less," https://www.hymnal.net/en /hymn/h/298.

DAY 80: UNEXPECTED DELIVERANCE

1. J. D. Barry et al, *Faithlife Study Bible* (Bellingham, WA: Lexham Press, 2012), digital download for use with Logos software at https://lexhampress.com/product/36338 /faithlife-study-bible.

DAY 82: MINDFUL OF GOD

1. Elisabeth Elliot, *A Chance to Die: The Life and Legacy of Amy Carmichael* (Ada, MI: Revell, 1987), 15.

DAY 93: UNDONE

1. Adapted from Gretchen Saffles (@gretchensaffles), "O Lord, I Have So Much to Do," Instagram, April 13, 2023, https://www.instagram.com/p/Cq-dHxNrg_K/.

DAY 94: SHE GAVE HER ALL; HE GAVE HER MORE

1. Christine Hunter, *Gladys Aylward: The Little Woman* (Chicago: Moody Publishers, 1970).
2. "Strongs #4657—*skybalon*," Blue Letter Bible, https://www.blueletterbible.org /lexicon/g4657/kjv/tr/0-1/.

DAY 98: WHAT DAY IS TODAY?

1. "C. H. Spurgeon: Psalm 118," Blue Letter Bible, https://www.blueletterbible.org /Comm/spurgeon_charles/tod/ps118.cfm.

INDEX

ABOUT THE AUTHOR

Gretchen Saffles is the founder of the global online women's ministry Well-Watered Women, the creator of the *Give Me Jesus* Bible study journal, and a passionate writer who longs to see women grasp the fullness of the gospel in everyday life. As a wife and mama, Gretchen has learned firsthand that just because your hands and days are full, it doesn't mean your heart has to be empty. Sharing her vulnerable life experiences, Gretchen writes with authenticity and boldness, encouraging women to seek Christ right where they are and live in his abundance.

Her journey began after college when she started working in youth and women's ministry at a church in Nashville. God used this time as a training ground to teach and grow her in her love for God's Word, and he gave her a passion to see women and girls know and delight in God's Word. After she got married and moved to Knoxville, Tennessee, she decided to take a leap of faith and begin an online shop and ministry called Life Lived Beautifully. Having no idea where to start, she started right where she was, with what she had: a small amount of money, a prayer journal, and a big dream stirring deep within her soul to encourage women to love Jesus deeply.

In 2014, God planted a fresh seed in her heart to create a Bible study journal for women to study God's Word. Through a series of God-ordained circumstances, the first *Give Me Jesus* journal launched in May of that year—and the initial batch of journals sold out within an hour. Since then, Gretchen's mission has been to create more Bible study resources and gospel-centered content to stir women's affection for Christ and equip them to know him more through his Word.

Gretchen changed the name of the ministry to Well-Watered Women to encompass the goal and mission of the ministry, founded on Isaiah 58:11. The mission of Well-Watered Women is to create engaging and theologically rich resources to grow women's love for God and his Word. Over the years, Gretchen has self-published several Bible studies, sold updated and revised versions of the *Give Me Jesus* journal, and created other guided journals and resources that walk women through various books of the Bible. She is the bestselling author of *The Well-Watered Woman* and *The Well-Watered Life*.

Gretchen lives in Atlanta with her husband, Greg, and their three children: Nolan, Haddon, and Emelyn. She loves going on adventures with her family, traveling to new places, daydreaming of wildflower fields, cooking tasty meals, baking chocolate chip cookies, painting, reading good books, and teaching women to know and love Jesus.

For more information on Well-Watered Women, visit the Well-Watered Women website and stay in touch through their social media pages. You can also follow Gretchen on social media.

WELLWATEREDWOMEN.COM

WELLWATEREDWOMEN

@WELLWATEREDWOMEN

@GRETCHENSAFFLES

DISCOVER THE BOTTOMLESS,
REFRESHING WELL OF GOD'S WORD
AND EXPERIENCE A FULLNESS AND
PEACE BEYOND YOUR CIRCUMSTANCES.

THE WELL-WATERED WOMAN

The Well-Watered Woman offers
spiritually hungry women tangible
tools to not only know Jesus more
but to live a life which thoroughly
enjoys him, seeks him, and follows
him into freedom.

978-1-4964-4545-2

THE WELL-WATERED LIFE

The Well-Watered Life
devotional journal is your
very own not-so-formal
invitation to embrace the
life Jesus came to give.

978-1-4964-4549-0

Available wherever books are sold.